GET SET GROW

MY EXPERIENCE WITH BUSINESS

SACHIN MOHAN CHOBHE

Made with ♥ on the Notion Press Platform
www.notionpress.com

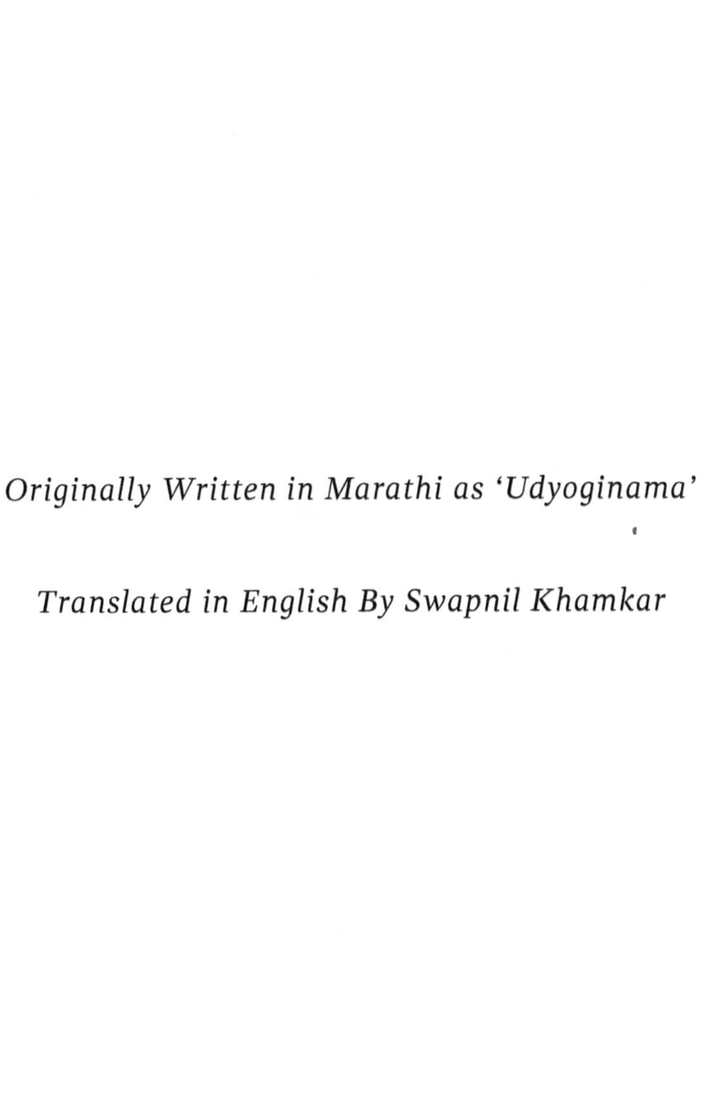

Originally Written in Marathi as 'Udyoginama'

Translated in English By Swapnil Khamkar

Contents

Acknowledgements

I dedicate this work to the ones who have made it possible for me to learn and grow:

To my parents, who have tirelessly provided me with the opportunity to learn through their hard work and sacrifices.

To my friends, brother, wife, and extended family members like aunts, uncles, and

grandparents, who have given me the strength to fight through life's challenges.

To the teachers, businessmen, and mentors who have inspired me to stay committed to my duties and shown me the path of continuous growth.

And to my partners, who, through their 'shocks' and experiences, have played a crucial role in shaping my journey and learning.

With utmost respect and gratitude, I dedicate this work to all of them.

About Author

Name: *Sachin Mohan Chobhe*

Author | Entrepreneur | Consultant

Education: MA-MCJ, MA (Defence & Strategic Studies) Savitribai Phule Pune University

Address: 06, Sai Complex, Sai Colony, Hanuman Nagar, Kedgaon Bhag (Ahmednagar), Ahilyanagar. Pin 414001

Email: sachin.chobhe@gmail.com

Business: Director, Devgro (OPC) Pvt. Ltd., Pune

Preface

What we write is either fictional or based on experiences we have lived. I have written in both categories so far. Many times, I have wondered whether I should write an autobiography. Perhaps it could be written in Marathi and English, and then into many other languages, reaching millions of readers, and I too could become famous. But like Mahatma Gandhi, I don't have the courage (or the merit) to present my own truth to the people. Similarly, like Arjuna, I do not have the mental readiness to fight against my own people, to share both good and bad experiences with the world. And it's not useful to write something useless like an autobiography. If I cannot tell the whole truth, what is the point of such a so- called 'autobiography'? For a long time, I had the thought of sharing my professional and social life experiences with readers in a different way, but I couldn't figure out how and when to start. I didn't even know what to write about. But eventually, a path was found, and this small book took shape.

In the forty years of my life so far, the social and professional success I have achieved is not something to boast about. But still, I have experimented, and I will continue to experiment. Just as Gandhi ji experimented with truth, I too have tried different things in my professional life. And I am still in the early stages. I have not yet reached the next stage of taking a leap after establishing myself in business (settling down, as we say in Marathi). However, some of my experiments have been successful, while others have been utterly unsuccessful. From being a labourer under the employment guarantee scheme to a journalist, writer, business consultant, and a small-scale businessman, my journey has been simple. Yet, there are many things I feel compelled to share as a 'human'. Many will like them, and many won't. Not everyone needs to like it, because every person's perspective is different when looking at anything. This perspective is determined by the experiences we have, the books we have read, and the surroundings we have assimilated.

Looking back at my birth and education in a village like Ruikhel (Tal. Shrigonda, Dist. Ahilyanagar), I am surprised myself. I was just an ordinary boy from a simple family. My parents gave me the opportunity to study, my uncles and grandparents gave me strength, and friends like Shashikant Mangade and Sunil Zagade showed me the path of reading. Then I came to Nagar (Ahmednagar). Relatives helped me. My younger brother Amit, who set aside his own education, worked hard to support me during my college days. Friends like Kishore Raktate, Anilbhau Chobhe, Ravi Haral, Shekhar Shinde, Ganesh Chobhe, Mahesh Chobhe, Nilesh Chobhe, Manoj Chobhe, Santosh Baraskar, Sachin Athre Patil, and many others like brothers gave me timely support and cooperation. Some gave me 'different experiences' that made me truly 'experience-tested' in life. These people became the real guides of my professional journey, and I am deeply grateful to them. While studying journalism at Marathwada Mitra Mandal College, Pune, Santosh Shenai sir gave me special attention and shaped me. Friends like Brijmohan Patil, Sukirt Gumaste, Niranjan Medekar, Deepak Kamble, Abhijit Barbhai, Madhuban Pingale, Ashokrajee Nimbalkar, Suresh Ingle, Suryakant Netke, Suryakant Varkad, Sahebrao Narsale, Ganesh Shendge, Gorakshnath Bandal, Uddhav Kalapahad (KP), Umesh Bhosale, Gangadhar Bansode, Mukund Bhalerao helped me in many ways. This is how I became who I am today.

I have met hundreds of people through my job and business. With some, I formed close ties; with others, I formed close and then broken ties. I take responsibility for my own faults in these matters because those who accept us with all our virtues and flaws stay with us, while others follow their own path. And we too do the same. Whenever I have faced failure in business or when someone has left me, one thing is clear: what did I do wrong? If you understand your mistake, correct it. If someone else has erred, forgive them. The key point is that change is the permanent nature of the universe. We, too, as human beings and professionals, are part of this nature. At such times, accept the opportunities and experiences with an open heart. Take the positive aspects, and leave behind the negative ones, and move forward with a new path or a new direction on the same road. Do not hold the thought that "if they did it, I will show them by doing the same." The world is much bigger than us. We are just a small and insignificant part of it. Give others the chance to bloom. While blooming yourself, do not let thoughts of competing with others to show off take root. Because, while money is important in business, and in life in general, personal satisfaction is equally important. Money is a tool, not the ultimate goal. Therefore, enter into business, trade, or entrepreneurship with an open mind. Earn good money. Spend it wisely. Avoid squandering it. Keep learning new things. Accept the experiences you encounter in a positive manner and make way for even more change.

It was Lokshahir Annabhau Sathe who instilled in me the love for reading. Shri. Na. Pendse's 'Garambi's Bapu' showed me a different path.

Dhruv Bhatt's 'Tatvamasi' guided me in a different direction. In professional life, I gained some maturity through the opportunities provided by Hanmant Rao Gaikwad, the chairman of BVG. Additionally, CA Rajendra Kale, AVGC's Vaibhav Dhasal, Yogesh Katare, retired Additional Chief Executive Officer Jagannath Bhore, former Deputy Chief Executive Officer Nitin Udmale, journalists Vithal Landge, Sudhir Lanke, Dr. Bharat Kardak, and many other friends and colleagues in the media sector guided me. It is through them that I became what I am today.

Throughout my career in business and professional life, I have met countless people. Some shared their journey and some, through their very experiences, shaped mine. It is these people I deeply thank for being a part of this journey. This is not a guide for those who already run a successful family business or for those whose families already have a stable business. They have the skills to teach their own. This book is for those who want to start something new, who want to step into business and earn their living, create a distinct identity for themselves, and contribute positively to society. This is a small attempt to share insights with them. Of course, this is not a perfect guide.

While writing this book, I was inspired by various professional writings and books. I had also read the books of renowned authors like Atul Kahate's Warren Buffet book. Kahate Sir was our teacher during our journalism course at Marathwada Mithramandal College of Commerce. The discussions we had with him on the college terrace were very helpful and inspired me to keep going. The influence of these writers and their books, and the responses they have received, motivated me to embark on a similar journey in Marathi. But the busy schedule at work delayed the final editing of this book, which resulted in this book reaching your hands much later than expected.

While I was busy in business, I never picked up any technical business books written in Hindi, English, or any special ones for professional guidance. I did read books, but none in the business genre. Now I realize that this was a mistake. However, I have read books by Shiv Khera and 'Rich Dad Poor Dad' by Robert Kiyosaki, as suggested by my friends, and watched motivational YouTubers who work in the business field. But I didn't find them much useful because they provide only surface-level and temporary inspiration. What I truly realized is that real understanding only comes when we take action. Business is such a field where, without action, nothing makes sense.

Through my articles in newspapers and various online platforms, I have absorbed small doses of professional knowledge. These small doses were enough to keep me updated. But I now realize that after the publication event of this book, I will need to explore such business literature further.

The idea of writing this book took at least five years to come to fruition. Initially, I thought I could write a book, but I questioned my own ability, competence, and experiences. The other question was: Who would even read it? However, over time, I wrote stories on platforms like 'Storytel', and the success story of BVG was published in the first-year Marathi textbook of the Savitribai Phule Pune University's Commerce Department. This encouraged me to continue, and once I saw that readers were interested in business advice, I started writing small pieces of advice. Writing this book has been a journey. It was initially just a hobby but gradually took the shape of something more serious. Many of my writings have been published in 'Lokmat' (Ahmednagar edition), which readers liked. They suggested new issues to explore, and this book began to take shape. Thus, the team at Lokmat and my guiding friends, like journalist Sudhir Lanke, played a major role in bringing this book to fruition.

Despite being involved in business, I haven't yet explored any professional business books deeply, but I certainly intend to explore more in the future, as I now realize the importance of doing so.

This book is not designed to give you the answers, but it aims to highlight the areas you may have missed, something you might find helpful in your business journey. It's a simple but heartfelt guide from someone who's learned from trial and error.

- Sachin Mohan Chobhe

CHAPTER ONE

From Mischievous to Entrepreneurial - A Pathway to Success

Many of us have encountered this sentiment, or perhaps even heard it firsthand: "That child was always so mischievous, and look where it got him—a successful entrepreneur!" These words are often uttered with a mix of surprise and admiration by those who marvel at the transformative journeys of individuals who began as average students but later achieved remarkable success in the business world. Indeed, our society is full of stories about so-called backbenchers or students once deemed "ordinary" who went on to build empires, excel in civil services, or make headlines in fields like MPSC or UPSC. Their tales, frequently celebrated in the media, evoke wonder, and for some, a tinge of envy. Yet, within our own families, how often do we hear discouragement or scepticism directed at anyone daring to tread an unconventional path?

In Maharashtra, a traditional mindset has long prevailed, one that places tremendous value on the security of a steady job. The common belief has been that a stable career is the most reliable way to ensure a bright future, and any deviation from this well-trodden path is typically met with caution or outright doubt. The deeply ingrained cultural preference for steady employment over entrepreneurial risk has kept generations anchored to the notion that success comes solely from secure, predictable careers. Parents, relatives, and elders often advise young people to pursue government jobs or positions in well-established companies, viewing these as the ultimate achievements.

However, the landscape is beginning to change, albeit gradually. With limited job opportunities and a globalized world offering diverse avenues, the idea of starting a business or embarking on an entrepreneurial journey is becoming more acceptable—and, for some, even necessary. The youth who once exuded a spark of "mischievousness," who may not have fit the mould of the "ideal student" but showed signs of creativity and innovation, are increasingly reconsidering entrepreneurship. This is not merely a romanticized notion but a response to a shifting reality, where the ability to innovate and adapt is more crucial than ever.

This evolution in mindset is essential. In today's rapidly changing world, entrepreneurship isn't just an option; it's an emerging necessity for anyone seeking self- sufficiency, influence, and personal growth. Those who dare to take a leap into business are gradually being celebrated, not ridiculed. Yet, even today, society has a tendency to underestimate or dismiss these backbenchers and self-proclaimed "mischievous" individuals. The predominant attitude remains sceptical, pigeonholing them as people who are unlikely to amount to anything of substance.

For generations, Marathi society has viewed education primarily as a means to secure employment, rather than as a way to cultivate curiosity, innovation, or independent thinking. This has contributed to a culture where anything other than a conventional career path is often met with apprehension. If a person, after studying, does not secure a job, the education system itself is blamed, and the individual is deemed a failure. What's often overlooked is the fact that genuine education should be a blend of theoretical knowledge and practical, applicable skills. It should encourage exploration and risk-taking, traits essential for entrepreneurship.

When one of these "average" or "mischievous" students succeeds in business, society's reaction is often tinged with sarcastic admiration. People express surprise, as if it's an anomaly, a disruption of the natural order. Yet these stories are what captivate public attention, for they break the societal norms and expectations that have been deeply ingrained over generations. These stories also offer hope and prove that unconventional paths can lead to extraordinary success.

Redefining Employment: From Job Seekers to Job Creators

In today's society, two prevalent ideas are often discussed and promoted: "Don't be job seekers; be job creators," and "Employment is enslavement;

business is freedom." While these motivational sayings have the potential to inspire, they can also mislead young people if taken too lightly or out of context. In the age of social media, an increasing number of so-called "inspirational speakers" and "motivational gurus" have emerged. Many of them make a living by selling dreams rather than offering real, actionable guidance. Their speeches and videos may ignite a temporary fire in people, filling them with enthusiasm, but rarely do they provide the necessary tools or steps required for sustainable success in business.

The truth is, many young people, without a clear sense of self-awareness or direction, get caught up in the fervour of these surface-level motivations. They dive headlong into business ventures, driven not by a well-thought-out plan but by the hype generated by motivational content. The result? Countless tales of failed businesses dotting our neighbourhoods, stories of young entrepreneurs who started with a spark of excitement but lacked the resources, skills, or knowledge to keep their ventures afloat. These failures become cautionary tales, reinforcing the already sceptical attitude toward entrepreneurship in Maharashtra. The fear of failure looms large, and this only deepens the existing mistrust of business as a viable career path.

Breaking the Cycle of Job Dependency

The cycle of fear, discouragement, and failure keeps Marathi society trapped in a loop of job dependency and a reluctance to embrace entrepreneurship. This cycle needs to be broken, and it requires a shift in both mindset and skill development. Young people must be encouraged not just to dream but to prepare rigorously and to build a foundation of practical, marketable skills. They need to be taught that success in business is not about blindly following a trend or getting swept up in the hype. It's about strategic thinking, continuous learning, and resilience.

My journey has taken me from being a highly educated worker confined by the security of guaranteed employment to a corporate advisor, and now to a business owner. Through this evolution, I've gained insights that I'm eager to share in this book. The aim of this book is to demystify entrepreneurship, breaking down complex concepts into relatable and understandable ideas. In our tech-savvy world, sharing positive, actionable ideas isn't just a choice; it's a responsibility.

The Power of Mindset: What You Think, You Become

One of the most talked-about concepts in personal development comes from the book 'The Secret', which asserts that "we become what we think about intensely." Such ideas are powerful, and they've been echoed countless times by motivational speakers. Yet, turning these thoughts into reality isn't as simple as daydreaming about success. For dreams to materialize, they must be grounded in consistent, deliberate action. If achieving goals were as easy as visualizing them, success would be universal. But as we all know, only a select few reach the pinnacle, leaving the rest to read about their achievements and wonder, "What's the secret?"

The reality is that true success requires immersing oneself in a chosen field, learning diligently, and putting in the necessary hard work. The Law of Attraction, made famous by The Secret, suggests that our thoughts and emotions influence our outcomes. While I've found some aspects of this philosophy valuable, particularly when accessed through platforms like YouTube and Spotify, I also recognize that it is incomplete on its own. Success is not a passive pursuit; it demands an active commitment to transformation and growth.

The Cycle of Inspiration, Action, and Experience

Real success stems from an interconnected cycle: inspiration ignites the flame, action keeps it burning, and experience shapes it into lasting achievement. Consider the Netflix film 'Srikant', which tells the compelling story of blind entrepreneur 'Srikanth Bolla'. His journey is a testament to the power of perseverance, resilience, and strategic thinking. Such stories serve as powerful reminders that success isn't about mere wishful thinking; it's about learning, adapting, and continuously striving to improve.

Our Thoughts Shape Our Reality

The central idea of 'The Secret'—that our thoughts shape our reality—holds merit, but only when coupled with unwavering self-belief and sustained effort. This concept is not just valuable for personal growth but crucial in the world of business. In entrepreneurship, maintaining a positive, goal-focused mindset can help sustain motivation even in the face of setbacks. Self-confidence builds trust, and when we believe in our vision, others, including potential clients and partners, are more likely to believe in us too.

Parents as Supporters, Not Masters

In Marathi society, parents often play a pivotal role in shaping their children's dreams, but this influence can sometimes become a limitation. Many parents harbour unfulfilled aspirations—perhaps they dreamed of becoming doctors, engineers, or IAS officers—and they project these dreams onto their children, regardless of the child's interests or strengths. This approach can be detrimental, creating a sense of frustration and even betrayal in the child.

True parental support lies in recognizing and nurturing a child's individuality. Instead of imposing traditional career paths, parents should guide their children to explore their interests, strengths, and passions. They should expose them to the right opportunities and support their choices, even if those paths seem unconventional. Communication is key, yet in many families, even among the educated, a significant gap persists. Bridging this gap is vital for the growth and happiness of future generations.

Gone are the days when every child was expected to aspire to become a doctor or engineer. Society has evolved, and so have the aspirations of the younger generation. Popular culture reflects this shift. For instance, 'Dil Chahta Hai' presented management as a viable and appealing career choice, moving away from traditional professions. Today, films like 'Pushpa' depict characters who pursue unconventional, even morally ambiguous paths to success. These portrayals resonate with audiences and suggest that society is more open to redefining what it means to be successful.

The Changing Definition of Success

This shift highlights the evolving cultural landscape, where the definition of success is no longer confined to safe, predictable careers. Parents must recognize this change and support their children in exploring diverse career options, whether they lie in entrepreneurship, the arts, or emerging technologies. Encouraging curiosity, resilience, and critical thinking will prepare the next generation for a world that is more dynamic and interconnected than ever before.

From Dreamer to Skilled Professional

Today's youth must go beyond fleeting dreams and embrace disciplined preparation. They need to understand that business is not a glamorous shortcut to wealth but a disciplined, strategic pursuit. The key is to move from being a dreamer to becoming a well-prepared, skilled professional. For those who meticulously plan and prepare for their entrepreneurial journey, the chances of success are far greater. The mindset should not be about hastily starting a business because it's trendy or because there are subsidies to be claimed. Instead, it should be about pursuing a well-thought-out vision with focus, adaptability, and resilience.

Give Wings to the Entrepreneurial Sky

So far, we have revisited various aspects of entrepreneurship, from being an mischievous child to becoming a successful entrepreneur. Of course, not all points have been covered because the world of entrepreneurship is vast, and my personal experiences, along with the insights I've gathered, are just a small part of it. One cannot simply compile experiences from across the world and declare, *"This is exactly how business should be done."*

Markets evolve constantly due to changes in technology, shifting consumer preferences, and, most importantly, the subtle transformations in human psychology. New ideas and consumer demands are born from this very process.

During my journalism studies in Pune, we had an insightful session on marketing by Professor Yogesh Pawale. His teachings have played a crucial role in shaping my practical understanding of the business world.

Beyond Passion: The Role of Environment and Support

Being passionate alone is not enough to transition from an idea to a successful business. The surrounding environment and the support of people also matter.

I recall a conversation from 2014-15 with my mentor and retired Agricultural Officer Prabhakar Tapkir, known for his farmer-centric approach. We were in Kolgaon (Tal. Shrigonda) covering a success story about curry leaf farmers. After gathering all the necessary information and photographs, our casual chat led to a discussion about his son.

He shared, *"My son Prashant was studying pharmacy, but he didn't like it. We wanted him to continue, which led to many arguments. However, these discussions were meant to find a solution, not to impose our will on him. Even today, I don't fully understand what he does—I just know it's something related to mobile advertisements. But I must admit, he has achieved greater success in his chosen field than we ever imagined. Now, we are proud of him."*

Like many families, Tapkir Sir's family believed that a stable job or, at most, a medical business was the ideal path to success. Most Indian families hold this belief firmly, thinking that walking the conventional path is the safest way to secure success. Given this mindset, it was natural for them to want Prashant to follow the same route.

However, the key difference was that they didn't forcefully stop him. Instead, they advised caution and supported his new venture. Prashant later founded "AdTreeva," a mobile advertising company. When I met him, I learned a lot about the IT sector. From a small city like Ahmednagar, he set up an office in a prime business tower and built a global network.

From Small Town to Media Empire

Another inspiring story is that of Tejas Shelar. A boy from Ahmednagar who runs the Ahmednagar Live 24 news portal. With limited technical knowledge, he entered the Marathi online media space and built his name.

When I first met Tejas in 2016-17, he and Sushil Shelke were just starting out. At that time, I had left my journalism job, had no salary, and was exploring goat farming while trying to establish an online news platform. I had previously attempted to register a weekly newspaper, *Krushirang*, but that failed.

I wanted to launch a news portal, so Tejas and Sushil offered to build one for me for   ₹10,000. However, since they did not have a business account at the time, I insisted on paying via cheque. This was a lesson I had learned after multiple business failures—proper financial documentation is crucial.

They accepted, opened an account, and developed Krushirang.com for me. From 2017 to 2022, that platform was my identity. However, despite having great content, I lacked technical knowledge. SEO, digital strategies, and online business tactics were beyond my grasp, and eventually, Krushirang.com began to fade out.

Tejas, on the other hand, mastered these skills. Today, he owns multiple news portals, YouTube channels, and earns a six-figure income monthly.

His family played a key role in his success, especially his mother, who, despite not fully understanding his work, never forced him onto a different path. Today, he stands tall as a leader in Marathi digital media.

Lessons from These Stories

These examples show that having knowledge is not enough; one must also have a well-rounded understanding of the field. What I couldn't achieve as a writer, Tejas managed in the media industry because he combined knowledge with practical execution.

Both Prashant and Tejas had the support of their families and friends, which allowed them to struggle, grow, and ultimately succeed. However, I have also seen highly intelligent individuals with excellent English and communication skills struggle because they failed to grab the right opportunities.

One of my favorite characters is Captain Jack Sparrow from *Pirates of the Caribbean*. He faces challenges with humour and confidence. While movies are fictional, the essence of his famous quote rings true:

"The problem is not the problem. The problem is your attitude about the problem."

In a recent discussion with Prafull Gadge and Umesh Bhosale, founders of BioMee, we compared business to painting. Just as an artist chooses a brush based on the canvas size, an entrepreneur must choose strategies based on market conditions.

My friend Kishor Raktate has often guided me and my friends on how to seize the right opportunities. His insights have been invaluable.

Leadership vs. Teamwork in Entrepreneurship

In 2016, when I quit my job, I had an illusion that I would single-handedly build an empire like Shivaji Maharaj and establish my own "Swarajya." However, after facing multiple failures, I had an eye-opening realization.

One day, former Government officer Nitin Udamale was speaking about a struggling entrepreneur and said:

"Not everyone is meant to be Shivaji. If you lack the capability to be a leader, then be a strong commander or a dedicated soldier. Only then can Swarajya be truly built."

This struck a chord with me. Instead of insisting on being the *king* in every endeavour, I started identifying leaders (Shivajis) in different fields and supporting them. Sometimes, I led from the front, while other times, I played the role of a team member. This mindset shift allowed me to explore multiple sectors—from tendering and trading to writing books, consulting institutions, and creating web series scripts.

Now, some of my friends jokingly ask, "Sachin, what exactly is your profession?" Because I have found my way in multiple domains.

Supporting Entrepreneurs: A Family's Role

Returning to the importance of family support, I recall an incident from 15 years ago. A friend moved to Ambegaon (Pune district) and began teaching in a school on a contractual basis. Later, he started a private coaching class, which was highly successful.

However, his family pressured him into preparing for a government job. He shut down his coaching business and eventually joined the police force. Despite earning a stable salary, he remains unsatisfied. Had his family believed in his vision, he could have built a top coaching institute.

This pattern repeats across industries—be it agriculture startups or IT businesses. Entrepreneurs who receive financial, social, and emotional support at the right time often create something extraordinary.

A Call for Change

We all love hearing success stories, but when it comes to helping struggling entrepreneurs, society often hesitates. Instead of offering financial aid or emotional support, they drown them in unnecessary advice.

If we want to truly nurture innovation in India, we need to foster a culture of social and financial backing for young entrepreneurs. Only then can we stop the cycle of missed opportunities and create a thriving business ecosystem.

CHAPTER TWO

Cultivating an Entrepreneurial Approach Through Continuous Learning

In today's rapidly evolving world, the allure of entrepreneurship captures the imagination of countless young individuals. A quick glance at social media, news articles, and motivational videos showcases the seemingly effortless lives of wealthy business magnates— highlighting luxury cars, glamorous vacations, and financial freedom. This curated portrayal creates a deceptive image that business success is easily attainable with nothing more than a sprinkle of ambition and a few basic resources. But in reality, entrepreneurship is far more intricate and requires far more than just enthusiasm. True business success hinges on the continuous development of a well-rounded skillset, mental resilience, and an unwavering commitment to both personal and professional growth.

Starting and sustaining a successful business is not just about a burning desire to succeed. It is about honing your mindset, learning from both triumphs and failures, and fostering an attitude of perseverance and adaptability. Many aspiring entrepreneurs fall into the trap of believing that successful business skills are inherited or that certain individuals are born with an innate "business mind." These myths are often perpetuated by widespread stereotypes—such as the notion that communities like Parsis, Jews, Jains, Marwaris, or Sindhis are naturally predisposed to excel in business. However, business acumen is not something that is genetically passed down; it is a cultivated skill, one that can be developed by anyone, regardless of their background, with time, experience, and the right mindset.

Exploring the Success of Certain Communities: A Cultural Foundation for Business Success

While it is true that some communities tend to excel in business, this success is often rooted in shared cultural values rather than innate talent. These communities have, over generations, nurtured a culture that deeply values mutual support, community-driven cooperation, and an unwavering commitment to mastering the necessary skills for entrepreneurship. Business success, within these groups, is viewed not as an individual pursuit but as a collective achievement—an effort where every member lifts each other and faces the challenges of entrepreneurship as a unified force. This spirit of cooperation, rooted in the belief that success is a communal effort, creates a fertile environment for business to thrive.

However, as the business landscape becomes increasingly inclusive, individuals from a variety of backgrounds are making their mark in the entrepreneurial world. People from farming communities, blue-collar professions, and previously marginalized groups are now establishing successful businesses. The key factor driving this transformation is a shift towards openness—a willingness to learn, adapt, and grow in a rapidly changing environment. The world of business is evolving, and as long as individuals remain open to education and growth, success is within reach for anyone willing to embrace the journey.

Embracing Interdependence: The Foundation of a Strong Business Mindset

A key trait of successful entrepreneurs is their understanding and acceptance of interdependence. There is often a misconception that independence means self-sufficiency— being able to handle everything on one's own. However, in reality, interdependence is the true cornerstone of sustainable success in both business and life. While we celebrate independence, society and business thrive on relationships and interconnectedness.

Think of a successful business as a living ecosystem, where every element plays an important role in the overall health and functionality of the system. This includes not just customers, but suppliers, partners, employees, and even competitors. It is this intricate web of interdependence that allows businesses to adapt, grow, and stay relevant in an ever- changing environment. For example, a business relies on its suppliers for raw materials, its customers for feedback and revenue, and its employees for expertise and innovation. The most successful entrepreneurs understand that no business can thrive in isolation—they work to nurture and strengthen these interdependent relationships, fostering trust, mutual respect, and loyalty in the process.

Business success is not the result of isolated efforts or singular achievement; it is the cumulative result of an ongoing process of building relationships with everyone involved in the business ecosystem. The most effective entrepreneurs recognize the value of partnerships and actively seek out individuals whose skills complement their own. Rather than focusing purely on self-sufficiency, they understand that collaboration fosters growth. They embrace the idea that successful partnerships and strategic alliances are often the catalysts for sustainable and mutually beneficial success.

Choosing the Right Business: Aligning Passions, Skills, and Market Potential

The process of selecting the right business idea is perhaps one of the most pivotal decisions an entrepreneur will ever make. Too often, individuals choose a business based on trends or the potential for financial gain, without considering whether the idea truly aligns with their passions, skillset, and long-term aspirations. The first step in building a successful business is to first have a deep and thorough understanding of what you want to achieve and why it matters to you.

Jumping into a business merely to impress others, or to meet societal expectations, is a surefire way to experience dissatisfaction and disappointment. Instead, the process should be deliberate. Take the time to research and reflect on your interests, strengths, and values. Gather insights from credible sources—industry reports, seasoned entrepreneurs, potential customers—and take the time to test your ideas before fully committing to them.

Sometimes, success lies in taking a slow, methodical approach rather than rushing in. Thorough preparation, reflection, and testing can often be the difference between building a sustainable business and one that falters early on. It is also crucial to learn from both successful and unsuccessful entrepreneurs. Those who have experienced failure can often provide invaluable insights into common pitfalls and mistakes, helping you avoid these traps in your own journey. Their experiences offer invaluable lessons in resilience, persistence, and the importance of constantly evolving in the face of challenges.

Once you have identified a potential business idea, take it for a test run. Engage with your target audience—whether friends, family, or strangers—and gauge their feedback. Does the concept resonate with them? Do they see value in what you are offering? These initial reactions can provide the necessary insights to help refine your ideas and turn them into a successful venture.

Confronting the Inner Enemy: Letting Go of Ego

Even after meticulous planning and preparation, there may come a time when you realize that your chosen business venture is not working out as expected. This is where the ability to pivot or even exit gracefully becomes crucial. Many entrepreneurs find themselves held back by their ego—the need to prove themselves to others, or the fear of being perceived as a failure. However, holding on to a struggling business out of pride or stubbornness is often more detrimental than accepting the reality and moving on.

In my own entrepreneurial journey, I've experienced both success and failure. Each venture has been a learning experience, teaching me valuable lessons in resilience, adaptability, and humility. Some businesses failed while others flourished, but each taught me something critical about the nature of success and the importance of adaptability. Over time, I came to realize that the most significant obstacle to success was not the market, nor the economy—it was my own ego. Learning to let go of my pride and focus on what truly mattered allowed me to make clearer decisions and prioritize value creation over personal validation.

This lesson is reflected in the experiences of many successful entrepreneurs who have faced setbacks and challenges. They understand that success is not about maintaining an unblemished record but about learning from mistakes, adapting, and continuously striving for excellence. As business expert Jim Collins wisely stated, "Good is the enemy of great." The path to greatness lies in the willingness to evolve, refine, and improve—embracing the changes necessary for long-term success.

Combining Creativity with Practical Skills

The most successful business ideas often begin as simple solutions to everyday problems. Take Amazon, for instance. What started as a modest online bookstore eventually grew into one of the largest e-commerce platforms in the world. Or consider Netflix, which originally began by mailing DVDs to customers and then revolutionized the entertainment industry by shifting to streaming services. These companies didn't begin with grandiose ambitions—they were built step-by-step, driven by a commitment to innovation and a relentless focus on customer satisfaction.

In the world of business, creativity is important, but it alone isn't enough. To truly succeed, creativity must be paired with practical skills and a deep understanding of the market. Too many aspiring entrepreneurs fixate on big, bold ideas while overlooking the critical aspects of execution. The real key to success lies in striking a balance between innovation and practicality. Your business idea should not only be creative but also feasible— addressing a real need in a way that is both unique and actionable.

Rather than attempting to launch something monumental from the get-go, focus on manageable steps that gradually build toward your larger vision. For example, if you're passionate about fashion, start by designing a small line of products rather than launching an entire brand. Test the market, gather feedback, and refine your approach. Over time, these small, consistent steps can lead to significant growth and help you refine your vision before scaling.

The Role of Continuous Learning in Business Success

A thriving business requires more than just knowledge—it demands a mindset of lifelong learning. In a marketplace that evolves at lightning speed, staying up-to-date with industry trends, consumer preferences, and emerging technologies is essential. This is especially true in fields like technology, where innovations occur daily. However, even in more traditional industries, the ability to adapt and keep learning is vital to remaining competitive.

Take Elon Musk, for example. Musk is known for his insatiable curiosity and his ability to immerse himself in complex subjects, from rocket science to electric vehicles to artificial intelligence. His commitment to continuous learning has empowered him to innovate across several industries, building some of the world's most influential companies. His example demonstrates that the thirst for knowledge is key to fostering the creativity and problem-solving skills necessary for entrepreneurial success.

It's also important to recognize that learning doesn't always come from formal education. While traditional degrees and certifications provide foundational knowledge, much of what you need to succeed in business can be gained through hands-on experience, networking, and self-study. Many of today's top entrepreneurs are self-taught, relying on books, online courses, and mentorship to build their skills and expand their expertise.

Calculated Risk and the Power of Adaptability

One of the most memorable lines in modern business is "Risk hai to ishq hai," popularized by the character of Harshad Mehta in a well-known TV series. This phrase captures the thrill of risk-taking, which is inherent to entrepreneurship. However, successful entrepreneurs understand that not all risks are created equal. The key is to take calculated risks—where the potential rewards justify the downsides, and strategies are in place to manage the unexpected.

Consider a small business owner looking to expand into a new market. Rather than pouring all their resources into this move, they might begin with a limited product launch or a short-term campaign. By analysing the results of this test, they can assess whether it's worth committing more resources. This approach not only minimizes potential losses but also provides valuable insights that can shape future decisions.

Adaptability is just as crucial. In the fast-paced world of business, even the best-laid plans can be derailed by unexpected events—economic downturns, shifts in consumer behaviour, or breakthroughs in technology. Entrepreneurs who can quickly pivot and adjust their strategies in response to such changes are the ones most likely to survive and thrive.

Balancing Knowledge with Practicality and Integrity

While knowledge is vital, it is not the only ingredient for success. Equally important are qualities like integrity, optimism, and a genuine desire to contribute to society. Business leaders who prioritize ethical behaviour and social responsibility often find that these values not only enhance their reputation but also help them build stronger, more lasting relationships with customers, employees, and partners.

Take Ratan Tata, for example, the former chairman of Tata Group, known for his ethical approach to business and his commitment to social causes. Tata's leadership was characterized by fairness, transparency, and respect for all stakeholders—from employees to the communities impacted by his companies. His reputation as a socially responsible business leader earned him widespread admiration that went far beyond financial success.

By combining knowledge with integrity, practical skills, and a focus on positive impact, entrepreneurs can create businesses that are not just financially successful but also socially beneficial. This holistic approach builds a sustainable foundation for long-term success, one that extends far beyond profits.

The Journey of Continuous Growth and Learning

Therefore, developing an entrepreneurial mindset and approach is a journey that requires commitment, self-reflection, and adaptability. Success in business isn't about shortcuts or instant results; it's about building a solid foundation of skills, relationships, and ethical principles that will carry you through both challenges and triumphs.

By embracing interdependence, selecting the right path, managing risks wisely, and remaining open to continuous learning, you can build a business that's not only profitable but also meaningful. Every step you take brings you closer to realizing your full potential and making a lasting impact on the world of entrepreneurship. As you continue along this journey, remember: success isn't just about achieving your goals—it's about creating something that resonates and endures in a constantly evolving world.

Look at the World with Open Eyes and Seek Opportunities

Having the right mindset does not automatically lead to success, nor does hard work guarantee a red carpet to prosperity. What truly matters is how well your perspective grows along with the current market and how effectively you assess the available opportunities over time.

You may have heard motivational speakers talk about Bisleri's story multiple times. When most Indians were still hesitant to spend money on Coca-Cola or Pepsi, this company introduced bottled water to the market.

To truly understand Bisleri's success, we must consider the situation at that time.

Bottled water entered the market by capitalizing on people's fear. In the 1970s, newspapers and newly emerging television channels focused on how contaminated water led to diseases. While some of these concerns were valid, they were not entirely factual. However, with constant media coverage, an unspoken fear took root in people's minds. An Italian company leveraged this fear and introduced Bisleri to India. Later, Indian entrepreneurs took over and made it a homegrown success.

Today, Bisleri is synonymous with bottled water. Whether it's a wedding, funeral, religious gathering, cultural event, or political function, 250ml or 500ml water bottles have become a standard part of meals.

I still remember that before 2005, even at the grandest of weddings, people drank regular tap water. Bottled water was considered a luxury. At that time, the price of pure milk was ₹12 per Liter, while a liter of bottled water cost ₹15. This pricing led to protests, with dairy farmers demanding that milk be priced at least as much as bottled water.

Over time, our access to resources has changed. In the early 2000s, simple dishes like *lapshi-sambar-rice* or *sheera* were considered food for the poor. Wealthier families served *boondi* at events, and *gulab jamun*—which is now easily available everywhere—was once a rarity.

India's economic liberalization policies, introduced by former Prime Ministers Narasimha Rao and Atal Bihari Vajpayee, and the expertise of economist Manmohan Singh, played a crucial role in uplifting the lower economic classes. Today, Prime Minister Narendra Modi continues this legacy by fostering startups and the "Make in India" movement, opening up new opportunities for innovation. We, too, must open our eyes and recognize these opportunities.

Data is Gold

A great example of leveraging data for business success is BioMee, a thriving startup in the agricultural sector, founded by Dr. Prafull Gadge. Their success is not just built on hard work but also on smart data utilization.

Team BioMee actively tracks research papers, government policies, and news updates to find solutions to farmers' problems. In the past five years alone, they have engaged thousands of farmers across India in agricultural literacy programs.

Dr. Gadge and his co-founder Umesh Bhosale often discuss market trends with me, staying updated on the latest developments in agriculture. I always say, "Data is gold," and they have turned this belief into reality by combining research with innovation to create unique agricultural products.

On a larger scale, tech giants like Google, Facebook, and Amazon have built their empires by capturing user data from mobile phones and emails. They track our online behaviour and generate enormous profits through targeted marketing.

Platforms like Facebook and Instagram have even played significant roles in political shifts, election outcomes, and corporate dominance. This proves that businesses must not only understand consumer needs but also analyse consumer behaviour and psychological patterns to stay ahead.

Some might think, *"I only run a small grocery store; how does this apply to me?"*

At first glance, this concern seems valid. However, based on my four years of experience in the retail business, I can confidently say that success isn't just about selling products—it's about strategic foresight.

For example, knowing in advance when festivals will occur, what natural disasters might impact supply chains, or how market trends will shift can make a significant difference.

During COVID-19, grocery stores became essential businesses because people feared food shortages. Similarly, a cyclone in Kerala can disrupt the coconut supply chain, leading to price spikes for coconuts and coconut-based products. Entrepreneurs who understand such market dynamics are the ones who maximize profits.

Nurture Your Talents and Skills

If you search on YouTube, you will find a movie called *Rang Rasiya*, based on the life of Raja Ravi Varma, a legendary painter. His story showcases how art transcends boundaries and speaks the language of the soul.

Ravi Varma was a rebel in his time, challenging societal norms through his work. His paintings were not just a means of entertainment but a powerful tool to question social, religious, and economic oppression.

What made him unique was that he approached art with a business mindset. His struggle to establish himself financially is depicted in the movie, and it is truly inspiring.

At that time, the King of Baroda, Sayajirao Gaekwad, provided him with financial and moral support, just as he had supported several intellectuals, artists, and entrepreneurs. Even today, when we start something new, we face both opposition and encouragement. It all depends on how we perceive people and when and how we connect with them.

Following a similar path, my friend Uddhav Kalapahad turned his love for anchoring into a full-fledged career.

Many people conduct wedding hosting as a hobby, but Uddhav took it to the next level. Instead of limiting himself to weddings, he explored other opportunities in the voice industry and is now recognized across Maharashtra as "Uddhav KP."

Similarly, my college friend Niranjan Medhekar built his storytelling and writing business by launching his own podcast company, "Sounds Great."

Another friend, Sukirt Gumaste, along with his wife Urmila Nimbalkar, successfully transitioned into full-time YouTubing.

Writer Nitin Thorat improved his craft and established himself as a leading young Marathi author. He even founded "Writer Publications," proving that authors can be financially independent if they adopt an entrepreneurial approach.

Learn from Others and Innovate

Examples of success are all around us—we just need to observe, analyse, and apply their strategies to our own business models.

If you are a writer, learn from Nitin Thorat. If you are a podcaster, study Niranjan Medhekar's journey. If you are interested in digital media, take inspiration from Tejas Shelar, who built a news empire from scratch.

Instead of blindly following trends, break down successful business models and adapt them to your strengths. This is how you find your unique path to success.

CHAPTER THREE

Choosing a Business Based on One's Capability

We've all heard the motivational phrases like, "Those who try, never fail." While there's certainly truth in the idea that perseverance is important, these statements often oversimplify the complex journey of entrepreneurship. Yes, trying is essential, but so is knowing your own limitations and capabilities. Many people, especially in the beginning stages of their entrepreneurial journey, get caught up in the fervour of copying the business models of others, without fully considering whether those models align with their own intellectual, physical, mental, and financial capacities. These factors play a pivotal role in determining whether a business venture succeeds or fails.

In this chapter, we will explore how crucial it is to choose the right business at the right time, and with the right resources. Success in business is not simply about motivation and ambition; it's about understanding your own limitations, being honest with yourself about what you can handle, and aligning those capabilities with the business you want to build. We'll dive into why blindly following trends or replicating someone else's success rarely leads to long-term success, and how practical realities must always be taken into account when making business decisions.

Let me share my own experience—an experience that profoundly shaped my understanding of the importance of aligning one's capabilities with business choices.

A Journey of Struggles, Setbacks, and Key Lessons

Early in my career, when I was still working as a journalist, I was filled with a burning desire to break free from the world of writing and reporting and venture into business. I had big dreams of becoming a successful entrepreneur, and I truly believed that with hard work and determination, I could achieve that success. However, like many aspiring entrepreneurs, I discovered that the road to business success is rarely as smooth as it seems.

I embarked on my entrepreneurial journey with two business ventures: one in the dehydration business and the other in business consultancy. Unfortunately, both of these businesses failed. Despite my efforts, both ventures could not take off the ground. But I wasn't discouraged—I refused to let failure define me. In fact, it was during this period that I learned some of my most valuable lessons about business.

What kept me going through these early struggles was the unwavering emotional and mental support from my family. Though we were not financially wealthy, my family stood by me, believed in me, and offered a sense of stability when everything seemed uncertain. Their support played a significant role in helping me remain persistent. It was during these difficult times that I realized how important it is to have a strong support system. Without the belief and encouragement of those around me, I may not have found the strength to keep trying.

After these initial failures, I was determined to try again. This time, I made the decision to leave my job and fully commit to entrepreneurship. I rented a small office in Bhutkarwadi, Savedi, Ahmednagar—just 100 square feet. It wasn't much, but it was a start. Despite the constant struggle to pay rent and keep the business afloat, I felt an unshakable drive to make it work. At this point, a few friends—including Mahadev Gavli—became partners in this new venture. Together, we tried to build something new in the food sector.

The Power of Ideas and Focused Conversations

Starting a business is often a whirlwind of ideas, plans, and strategies. I can't help but compare the experience to a quote from Game of Thrones: "The war begins with discussions of war." In business, the foundation of any venture is built on intense discussions and brainstorming. But, as I would soon learn, not all discussions are created equal. The direction and focus of those discussions can make or break the venture. In our case, the discussions were a bit too scattered at first. Everyone was enthusiastic, but we hadn't clearly defined the path forward.

While I was simultaneously working with NABARD on a project called "Water is Life", which spanned over 150 villages in the district, it inspired me to think about a business that could have a greater social impact. I envisioned a business that catered to farmers and women's self-help groups—offering fast-moving consumer goods (FMCG) at fair, reasonable prices. My goal was ambitious: to build a business that could compete with industry giants like D-Mart. My partners and I were excited about the idea, but as is often the case in business, things didn't go as smoothly as we had hoped.

Despite my successes in other ventures, I allowed myself to become distracted by the excitement of this new idea. I failed to assess whether we had the resources and strategies in place to compete with established giants in the market. And that's where we went wrong.

The Challenges of a "Copy-Paste" Business Model

The problem with many aspiring entrepreneurs, including myself at that time, is that we often fall into the trap of replicating successful business models. Our thinking becomes limited to copying what has worked for others without fully understanding the systems, strategies, or resources that made those businesses successful.

For instance, we thought we could replicate the success of D-Mart by opening our own store selling products from women's savings groups and farmers at fair prices. On paper, this idea seemed perfect. We even envisioned a store that combined a grocery store with a small restaurant offering unique, local dishes like shipi-amti.

But here's the reality: Finding the right space for our venture took over two months of intense searching. When we finally secured a location in Nalegaon, it wasn't as ideal as we had imagined. Despite this, we pressed forward. We launched our store under the names Lokrang Mega Mart and Lokrang Food Mart. To compete with the big players, we utilized social media and tried to position ourselves as a direct competitor to D-Mart.

Our next big mistake came with the decision to add a tea-and-snacks section to our business. Instead of focusing solely on groceries, we decided to diversify. The idea was to sell premium products from women's groups, along with fresh, local snacks like tea and regional delicacies. But despite all our enthusiasm and efforts, things didn't go according to plan.

Learning from Mistakes: The Importance of Focus and Financial Prudence

Our business model was flawed from the start. We were too focused on replicating what others had done without considering whether we had the resources, systems, or market understanding to do the same. Our first mistake was with pricing. Initially, we set the price of tea at 10 rupees, but one of the nearby tea stall vendors convinced us that 5 rupees would be a better price for the area. We agreed to drop the price to 7 rupees, and later to 5 rupees. But this pricing strategy didn't cover our costs. The quality of our tea suffered, and as a result, the business became unprofitable.

This led to significant losses—around 50,000 rupees—which we could not recover from. Our partners and I, despite our hard work and dedication, couldn't turn the business around. I also shifted focus to home delivery services for groceries, but even that didn't work out. There was too much movement without a clear, focused plan.

Then, the pandemic hit. Just as we were hoping to expand by bringing in new partners, the unforeseen challenges of COVID-19 hit hard. On top of this, my young daughter fell seriously ill, which added to the emotional toll. In just a month and a half, our business collapsed. We faced a loss of nearly 20 lakhs, along with three and a half years of effort spent building something that ultimately failed.

The emotional fallout was immense. I remember sitting by the side of the road with my wife on the night before Dussehra, tears streaming down my face. But it was in that moment of despair that I felt the deep strength of my family. Their support became the cornerstone of my ability to rebuild.

The Lessons Learned: Focus, Support, and Honest Self-Assessment

Looking back, I realize how important it is to focus on one thing at a time. I had jumped from one idea to another, without dedicating myself fully to any single venture. I also learned that a strong support system is essential. My family, despite the hardships, remained a pillar of strength.

The most important lesson, however, was that starting a business requires honest self- assessment. Before diving into any business, it's crucial to evaluate your mental, physical, and financial capacity. Are you truly ready for the journey ahead? Do you have the resources to weather the inevitable challenges? Are you prepared to face the setbacks and learn from them?

The Right Business, the Right Time, and the Right Resources

The key takeaway from this journey is simple but profound: when choosing a business, you must consider your capabilities—your skills, your resources, and your mental and emotional preparedness. Avoid the temptation to follow trends or jump into businesses that don't align with your abilities. Business success is a long-term endeavour that requires focus, hard work, and the right resources.

It's okay to start small, to test the waters before diving in headfirst. Starting a business doesn't mean you have to go big from day one. Focus on the long-term vision and keep your resources in mind. If you have the right support, the right resources, and the right mindset, you can ensure steady growth and build a business that is both sustainable and meaningful.

A Best Manager is Not Necessarily the Best Businessman

Let me share a story about a close friend of mine that ties directly into our discussion. Back in college, this friend of mine was a powerhouse. He excelled academically, and everything he did was marked by precision and dedication. After graduation, he went on to become my boss at a well-established company, and once again, he was exceptional. He had the knack for leadership and was brilliant at managing the complexities of running a business. Under his leadership, several companies grew from millions in valuation to billions. His skills in management were outstanding—if you asked anyone, they would say, "Hats off to him."

But despite all of his managerial success, my friend tried to start a business on his own— not once, but two or three times. He even quit his well-paying job to focus on his ventures. On paper, he had everything you would think he'd need to succeed in business—capital, experience, management skills, and a strong professional network. Yet, despite all of these advantages, his ventures didn't succeed. There's no need to get into the specifics of how each of those ventures panned out, but the bottom line is that they all ended in failure.

Interestingly, I mentioned him briefly in an article for Lokmat, a popular Marathi newspaper. When he read it, he reached out to me with a message that said, "You really hit the nail on the head. I've learned a lot from this."

His response was an acknowledgment of the one key insight I was trying to convey—just because someone excels in management doesn't mean they're naturally suited for entrepreneurship. This is what I want to emphasize here: Being the best manager doesn't automatically make you the best businessman. The two skills are vastly different, and simply replicating what's worked for others doesn't guarantee success.

Management and Entrepreneurship: Two Different Worlds

Many people, especially those with strong managerial experience, often fall into the trap of believing that because they are excellent at managing people and processes, they can easily transition into business ownership. It's a common misconception. The skills that make someone a great manager—whether it's controlling a team, managing operations, or increasing productivity—are not the same as those required to run a business from the ground up. Managing a business's operations is very different from being the person who carries the full responsibility for the business's success or failure.

For example, a manager's role is often to ensure that things run smoothly, within the systems and strategies set by others. But when you're an entrepreneur, you are the one who creates the system, makes the strategic decisions, and bears the responsibility for the consequences. There's a big difference between managing within a well-established framework and building a framework from scratch.

My friend's inability to transition from being a manager to a business owner wasn't due to a lack of skill or knowledge. Rather, it was because he didn't possess the mentality or mindset of a business owner. It's a mindset that involves risk-taking, patience for growth, long- term thinking, and an ability to absorb failure without losing momentum. Entrepreneurship requires a willingness to pivot and try different approaches, often without a clear roadmap. It's a reality that is far removed from the more structured, predictable world of management.

Risk Management: The Unsung Hero of Success

Now, here's another crucial aspect of business success that is often overlooked—risk management. Some of the most successful entrepreneurs may not have the best knowledge or expertise, but they have an innate ability to take calculated risks. Success in business, whether it's in the corporate world or small startups, isn't just about having the best knowledge or the most experience. It's about understanding risks, managing them, and leveraging the existing skills you have to mitigate those risks.

This doesn't mean that you should jump into business without knowledge or planning. Far from it. What I'm emphasizing here is that many people mistakenly believe that everything must align perfectly for success to happen. They believe that if you have all the knowledge, resources, and support, success is guaranteed. But the reality is that the most successful people in business often achieve their success not by avoiding risk, but by learning how to manage it effectively.

Whether in business, politics, or any other field, understanding the risks involved and knowing how to handle those risks is often what separates successful entrepreneurs from those who fall short. You can't always rely on everything falling into place. In fact, it rarely does. Success often comes from being able to adapt, to learn from your mistakes, and to keep moving forward despite the challenges.

The Illusion of External Support

It's also important to recognize that while external help can be valuable, you cannot depend on it to drive your success. Many people enter business with the false hope that a family member or a friend will help them succeed, making promises like "I'll help you become a millionaire." These assurances can be tempting, but they're often misguided.

Yes, a bit of support can be useful, and it can provide a safety net in the initial stages. But ultimately, the business is your responsibility, and you alone are responsible for its success or failure. Many entrepreneurs begin with the belief that external help will be enough to carry them to the top, only to realize that they must confront the realities of business on their own.

This is where the true essence of entrepreneurship lies—the learning, the challenges, the mistakes, and the eventual growth. External help might make some things easier, but it's your own ability to adapt, learn, and grow that will define your success in business.

Business is About More Than Skill—It's About Attitude

The key takeaway from this chapter is that business is not just about having the right skills; it's about the right attitude, the ability to take calculated risks, and the willingness to learn from failure. Just because you're a great manager doesn't mean you'll automatically be a great business owner. The skills and mindset required to manage a team or company are different from those needed to run your own business.

In business, you must learn to embrace failure, understand your own limitations, and continually refine your strategy. Don't be afraid to take the plunge, to step into the arena, and to try your best—even if that means facing failure along the way. It's through those failures that you learn the most valuable lessons about what works and what doesn't.

In the end, it's your readiness, your resilience, and your willingness to take on risks that will determine your success. It's not about copying others or relying solely on external help— it's about honing your own abilities, managing your own risks, and continually learning from both success and failure.

Success is Personal

Success in business doesn't come from imitating others, and it doesn't come from relying solely on external factors. It comes from understanding your own capabilities, managing risks wisely, and developing the mindset of a true business owner. While inspiration can be drawn from others, it's your own readiness, attitude, and capacity to face the challenges head-on that will truly define your success in the business world.

So, don't be afraid to take that leap. Understand your risks, be prepared for failure, and take responsibility for your own journey. Only then will you know whether you have what it takes to succeed, and only then will you grow into a true entrepreneur.

Avoid Stubbornness; Embrace Effortlessness

My friend Kishor Raktate has often guided us through tough times, offering fresh perspectives and helping many of us grow. He frequently reminds us not to cling stubbornly to any idea or decision because that kind of rigidity often leads us down the wrong path. Instead, he advises making choices that feel natural, ensuring they don't cause undue stress to ourselves, our families, or society.

We often hear inspiring success stories where people emphasize how they struggled and endured hardships to achieve their goals. While these stories deserve respect, who has ever truly escaped struggle?

Kishor once put it humorously:

"Even Mukesh Ambani's children couldn't freely play in the open like regular kids—that too is a kind of struggle for them!"

As ordinary people, we can roam around freely, enjoy simple pleasures, and make independent choices—something that's not always possible for the children of business tycoons like Ambani and Adani. Their life canvas is different, their challenges unique, and they, too, face struggles in their own way.

So, should we constantly magnify our hardships? I, too, have spent nights sleeping at Swargate Bus Stand, survived on vada pav, and faced my share of struggles during college. But what matters is not showcasing hardships, but learning from them and growing stronger.

Even now, while writing this book, I am suffering from sciatica pain. Does that mean I should start sharing my struggles and charging fees as a motivational speaker?

The answer is NO.

Becoming a "motivational speaker" might bring money and political connections, but do I have the skills for it? Exaggeration and dramatic storytelling aren't my strengths, so it's clear that I wouldn't succeed in that profession. That's why it's crucial to identify our true skills before choosing a career or business.

Just because someone else is succeeding in a particular field doesn't mean we should copy them. Avoid making blind comparisons like:

- *He bought that car, so I should too.*
- *He built a big house, so I must have one as well.*
- *If he is succeeding in a certain business, I should enter that field too.*

Instead, focus on the business or profession that suits you, approach competition with an open mind, and stay dedicated to your chosen path. I once entered the grocery business without proper knowledge or the willingness to adapt. Naturally, I failed. We need to identify our strengths and weaknesses before making business decisions. Some people think, *"My relative or friend knows how to run this business, so I'll just partner with them."* But if you lack the necessary expertise, adaptability, and commitment, failure is inevitable.

Be Ready to Exit When Necessary

We are living in the early days of Artificial Intelligence (AI), and in the coming years, we will witness huge, unpredictable changes in business and technology. India is not yet a major player in AI development, but we are rapidly adopting it.

Out of curiosity, I once asked ChatGPT to generate an article on "descriptive article on history of tata groups closing project or companies in Marathi language." To my surprise, the AI provided an insightful, detailed article listing Tata's business failures. This shows that choosing the right business is important, but recognizing when to exit is equally crucial. Even Tata Group, which acquired Jaguar and Land Rover, had to shut down or exit multiple businesses over time.

A historical example is the Dunkirk Evacuation, where British and French forces strategically retreated, saving 325,000 soldiers. This retreat later helped them regroup and defeat Hitler's forces.

Similarly, Tata Group has experienced ups and downs since its founding in 1868. They wisely exited loss-making projects like:

- The Nano Car Project
- Tata Coffee retail ventures (before partnering with Starbucks)
- Tata Teleservices, which was sold to Airtel in 2017 due to rising competition and financial losses

On the other hand, companies that failed to exit at the right time collapsed.

For example:

- Future Group's "Big Bazaar" stores failed due to mismanagement and were later acquired by Reliance Retail.
- Meanwhile, D-Mart thrived by maintaining strong financial discipline and strategic expansion.

Some business owners refuse to shut down failing ventures out of fear:

- *"What will people say?"*

- *"My relatives will mock me!"*
- *"Will I be labelled a failure?"*

This unnecessary pressure leads to severe financial losses and even suicides among entrepreneurs. A new trend is emerging—just as MPSC aspirants once dominated conversations, now everyone claims to be working on a startup. While startups are great, blindly jumping into business without proper planning is dangerous. Just as failed farmers blame agriculture, failed startups could damage the reputation of entrepreneurship itself.

The Tragic Story of Café Coffee Day's Founder

Starting a business doesn't guarantee success. It requires vision, strategy, and adaptability.

V.G. Siddhartha, the founder of Café Coffee Day (CCD), launched India's first large-scale coffeehouse chain with the perfect marketing strategy. However, he later expanded into unrelated sectors and struggled to manage the growing business. When financial mismanagement and rising debts became overwhelming, he ended his life—a tragic loss for Indian entrepreneurship. However, CCD as a business survived. By shutting down loss-making outlets and focusing on profitable ones, the company regained stability.

The key takeaway: Exiting from failing ventures is not a defeat—it is a strategic move.

Business Is About Smart Decisions, Not Stubbornness

If you choose a business just because others are doing well in it, you may struggle.

Instead, study successful business models, adapt them to your strengths, and stay open to changing strategies when necessary.

- Avoid blind competition.
- Do not let ego drive your business decisions.
- Know when to hold on, and know when to let go.

This is how smart entrepreneurs build lasting success.

CHAPTER FOUR

If You Stop, You're Finished... But If You Persist, You Will Succeed

The phrase "If you stop, you're finished" is one of the most powerful and universally relevant truths in both business and life. It's not just a catchy saying—it's a guiding principle that should govern how we approach every aspect of our lives. In school, at work, in business, or in personal growth, if you pause for even a moment, you risk falling behind. Life and the world around us don't wait for anyone. If you stop moving forward—whether mentally, physically, or professionally—you will quickly find yourself obsolete.

In the business world, we can see countless examples of companies and individuals who failed because they stopped evolving. Businesses that were once industry giants have vanished simply because they failed to keep up with changing times and innovations. Take the example of companies like Kodak, Blockbuster, and even Yahoo. At one time, these companies were kings in their fields. But their inability to adapt to new technologies, changes in consumer behaviour, and shifts in market demands led to their decline. Similarly, individuals who were once successful can find themselves irrelevant if they cease evolving with their industries.

This concept is true not only in business but in all walks of life. Think about education. If a student stops studying, stops learning, or stops seeking new knowledge, they will fall behind their peers. It's the same in sports—if an athlete stops training, they risk losing their competitive edge. In the workforce, if a person stops improving their skills or adapting to new tools and methodologies, they will soon find themselves replaced by someone more current, more innovative.

The key takeaway here is simple: never stop. The real growth in life comes from continuous learning, the willingness to adapt to change, and the persistence to keep moving forward. Whether you're running a business, building a career, or pursuing personal growth, those who keep pushing forward—embracing challenges, adapting to change, and constantly striving for improvement—are the ones who will succeed in the long run.

The Power of Persistence: The Story of Dhirubhai Ambani

A prime example of someone who exemplified the importance of persistence and forward momentum is Dhirubhai Ambani, the founder of the Reliance Empire. Dhirubhai didn't come from wealth or privilege. He started with nothing, but through sheer determination, vision, and relentless work ethic, he built one of the most powerful and influential business empires in India—and the world. His journey is a testament to the power of persistence and the importance of always moving forward.

Dhirubhai Ambani didn't just build a company; he built a legacy. His company, Reliance, continues to shape industries and impact millions, even after his passing. Ambani's success wasn't just about having a great idea; it was about his ability to persist despite overwhelming odds. He faced numerous challenges, including fierce competition, financial difficulties, and even political hurdles. But he never stopped. He understood that business is a journey, not a destination. And to succeed, you must keep evolving, keep innovating, and never rest on your past achievements.

Ambani's story teaches us an important lesson: never stop striving. Just because things are going well doesn't mean you should stop. Success is not the endpoint—it's the continuous pursuit of growth and improvement that leads to lasting success. Ambani's story is a reminder that resting on your laurels will only lead to stagnation.

The Split of the Ambani Brothers: A Lesson in Adaptability and Choices

When Dhirubhai Ambani passed away, I was still in college, and his story had a profound impact on me. After his death, the Reliance group was divided between his two sons, Mukesh and Anil Ambani. Both sons had similar opportunities, resources, and inheritances, but their paths have been very different. Mukesh Ambani, who took over the telecommunications division of Reliance, embraced new opportunities, adapted to the rapidly changing market, and made bold, innovative decisions that disrupted the telecom industry in India. His decision to launch Reliance Jio revolutionized the telecom landscape and brought immense global recognition to the company.

On the other hand, Anil Ambani faced several challenges that led to a sharp decline in his businesses. Despite having the same resources, Anil Ambani made different choices. He failed to adapt to the changing business environment in the same way his brother did. Mukesh's willingness to innovate, take risks, and keep moving forward resulted in his success, while Anil's inability to do the same led to a decline in his business empire.

This contrast between the two brothers underscores a crucial lesson: success is not just about what you start with; it's about the choices you make along the way. Even with equal opportunities, success ultimately depends on how you respond to the challenges you face and whether you're willing to adapt and evolve. Mukesh's ability to stay forward-focused and embrace new opportunities demonstrates the power of persistence and adaptability in business.

The Road to Success: Persistence, Adaptability, and Innovation

For over twenty-five years, I have studied the rise and fall of both brothers' companies. From this experience, I have learned an invaluable lesson: success is not guaranteed, even with the best resources. The road to success is paved with persistence, adaptability, and the ability to keep moving forward, even when things are difficult. When things are going well, it can be tempting to relax, to enjoy the success you've achieved. But that's exactly when stagnation sets in. Comfort breeds complacency, and complacency breeds failure.

In business, education, or any aspect of life, growth is an ongoing process. It requires continuous effort, learning, and the willingness to adapt to new circumstances. If you stop learning, if you stop innovating, you risk losing your edge. Complacency is your greatest enemy, and progress is your best ally. Whether you're building a business, a career, or simply trying to improve yourself, never stop. Never stop seeking knowledge, never stop innovating, and never stop improving. Only then will you thrive.

The key to success, then, is simple: keep going. Keep moving forward, keep pushing through challenges, and keep striving for improvement. Success is not an end point—it's a continuous journey. And it's only those who embrace that journey, who continue to learn, adapt, and grow, who will ultimately succeed.

Thrive Through Persistence

Therefore, if you want to succeed, you must embrace the idea that the journey is never truly over. Whether it's in business, education, or personal development, growth is a continuous process. The moment you stop striving, you risk being left behind. Embrace persistence, adaptability, and innovation, and never stop improving. Life will continue to move forward, and if you keep up with it, you will not just survive—you will thrive.

The Larger Market Is Bigger Than Local Rivalries

Whether we come from a small village or a bustling city, the desire for success is universal. In smaller communities, this drive is often accompanied by the pressure to prove ourselves—to our friends, family, and neighbours. We start to measure our success by comparing ourselves to those around us. However, there is a dangerous pitfall here: when we become overly focused on outshining others within our local sphere, we lose sight of the larger opportunities that lie beyond. Local rivalries, or what can be called "village politics," can cloud our judgment and limit our potential. To achieve true success, we must expand our focus and aim for the larger market.

Many people start off strong in business, but their growth is hindered by an excessive focus on local competition. They become so preoccupied with proving that they are better than their peers or neighbours that they forget to look beyond the confines of their immediate surroundings. This narrow mindset, while often tempting, can severely restrict the potential for long-term success.

The Trap of Local Rivalries: A Personal Story

I remember a friend of mine who embarked on a business venture related to Ayurvedic health products about twenty years ago. During this time,

Ayurvedic health practices were gaining significant popularity, especially with the rise of Baba Ramdev's yoga camps and his widespread promotion of herbal remedies. Inspired by this trend, my friend began supplying Ayurvedic powders and dehydrated vegetables to suppliers in larger cities like Pune and Mumbai.

Initially, his business flourished. He quickly established himself as a reliable supplier and saw success. He bought a car, a house, and expanded his operations. For a while, everything seemed to be going well. However, as his success grew, so did his ego. Rather than focusing on expanding his business and catering to a broader market, he became more interested in showcasing his achievements to his local community. His desire to flaunt his success and assert his dominance in the neighbourhood began to overshadow his focus on the business itself.

At some point, he got entangled in local politics. This involvement, driven by his inflated ego, started to affect his judgment and decision-making. He began making choices that were more about proving a point to those around him than about fostering long-term business growth. As a result, he lost valuable business connections, alienated friends, and ultimately, his business crumbled. The same community that once celebrated his success turned against him. His once-thriving venture withered, and he was left with nothing but regret.

Looking back, it's clear that had he focused on the larger market—on expanding beyond the local competition—he could have achieved far greater success. Instead, he became trapped in small-town rivalries and let his ego dictate his business decisions. This is a classic example of how unchecked ego and a narrow focus can derail even the most promising ventures.

The Importance of Focusing on Growth, Not Rivalries

In business, the key to success is not how well you outshine those around you in your local community. Your true success is defined by your ability to scale, build a sustainable business, and adapt to a broader market. Focusing on outdoing your local rivals may bring temporary satisfaction, but it limits your potential in the long run.

A successful business thrives when it looks beyond local borders. It seeks opportunities for growth, diversifies its reach, and continuously innovates to meet the needs of a larger, global market. By focusing on personal competition or local rivalries, you risk losing sight of what's important: building something with long-term potential, something that can create real impact and bring real value to the world.

Ego-driven decisions often cloud judgment. They lead people to prioritize immediate recognition or victory over lasting progress. The satisfaction of winning a local rivalry may seem appealing, but the true reward lies in building a business that outlasts such temporary victories.

The Bigger Picture: Growing Beyond Local Boundaries

To achieve sustainable success, it's essential to break free from the chains of local rivalries. Whether you're in a small town or a large city, remember that the world is much bigger than your immediate surroundings. The larger market—whether national or international—is full of opportunities waiting to be explored. It's in this larger space that true success resides.

If my friend had shifted his focus from local politics to expanding his business into other markets, he might have seen his Ayurvedic products reach a global audience. By understanding the power of growth beyond the familiar, he could have transformed his business into a lasting enterprise. But because he chose to invest in ego-driven decisions, he lost sight of the bigger picture.

Business, like life, is about playing the long game. If you want to succeed, don't get caught up in small-town rivalries or ego battles. Instead, focus on building something that can reach farther, make a greater impact, and leave a lasting legacy. The true potential of your business lies not in competing with your neighbours, but in creating a product or service that resonates with a larger, more diverse audience.

Shift Focus to the Larger Market

The lesson here is clear: don't get bogged down by local rivalries or the pressure to compete with those around you. While it's natural to compare yourself to your peers, true success lies in expanding your vision. Build a business that can grow beyond your immediate community. Focus on the larger market, innovate, and embrace opportunities for expansion. It's only by looking beyond local borders that you can create something meaningful and lasting.

As you strive for success, always remember: the larger market is far bigger than any local rivalry. Don't let small battles limit your potential—expand your vision, embrace the opportunities that come your way, and build a business that can thrive on a global scale.

Business Is Bigger Than Ego

"Business is bigger than ego." This powerful statement captures one of the most significant truths in the world of entrepreneurship. Ego, though often subtle and hard to recognize, can be one of the biggest barriers to long-term success. Many entrepreneurs start strong, full of ambition and determination. But as they achieve success, they may fall victim to their own inflated sense of self-importance. They start to believe that their way is the only way, that they are infallible, and that no one can challenge them. It is at this point that ego takes over—and that's when things can go wrong.

Ego often blinds us to our flaws, prevents us from acknowledging mistakes, and prevents us from learning from the challenges we face. In business, when the driving force behind decisions is ego, failure becomes inevitable. This is because business requires adaptability, humility, and the ability to learn and evolve. If ego takes centre stage, it becomes impossible to navigate the inevitable changes in the marketplace.

A Cautionary Tale: The Fall of a Business Empire

I remember a friend of mine who once ran a flourishing business with a turnover of over 150 crores. His business was thriving, and everything seemed to be going according to plan. He had built a solid foundation and was moving toward even greater success. However, as his business grew, so did his ego. He became overly confident and started to think that he had mastered the market. Instead of focusing on further growth, he became obsessed with asserting his dominance in the industry.

At some point, his mindset shifted entirely. His attitude morphed from focusing on customer satisfaction and innovation to focusing on proving his superiority. "We are the kings of the market," he would say. But this arrogance came at a cost. His focus on ego-driven decisions began to overshadow the strategies and innovations that had once driven his business to success. He stopped paying attention to the changing market dynamics, believing that his previous success would always carry him forward.

Ultimately, his downfall wasn't due to a lack of resources or a declining market—it was the result of decisions fuelled by ego. He lost touch with the very principles that had made his business successful in the first place. The market moved on, competitors adapted, and he failed to keep up. What had once been a flourishing empire slowly started to unravel, all because his ego led him to believe that he could not be defeated.

This story highlights the danger of letting ego drive your business decisions. It is easy to become complacent and overconfident when things are going well. But business is not just about winning battles; it's about adapting to new challenges and staying grounded. The most successful entrepreneurs are not the ones who think they know everything—they are the ones who remain humble, continue to learn, and are always ready to change course when necessary.

The Key to Success: Humility and Adaptability

The true key to business success is to never let your ego dictate your decisions. Humility, learning, and adaptability are what separate successful entrepreneurs from those who fall prey to their own arrogance. When you remain humble, you open yourself up to new ideas and perspectives. You stay grounded and aware of the ever-changing landscape of business.

A business that is driven by ego will eventually be blindsided by reality. Markets evolve, consumer preferences shift, and new challenges arise. Those who let their ego get in the way are the first to miss these signs. On the other hand, entrepreneurs who are willing to acknowledge their weaknesses, accept constructive criticism, and evolve with the times are the ones who will thrive in the long run.

Business Is a Long-Term Commitment

Another crucial lesson in business is that success does not come overnight. Business is not a sprint; it is a marathon. It requires patience, perseverance, and the ability to bounce back from setbacks. Every entrepreneur will face challenges, and at times, the road ahead will seem difficult and uncertain. But the key is to keep going. Success in business is not about avoiding failure; it's about learning from it and continuing forward despite it.

Building a business is a long-term commitment. There will be highs and lows, but those who persevere through the tough times are the ones who will ultimately succeed. In fact, some of the most successful entrepreneurs in the world have faced significant failures along the way, only to turn them into stepping stones toward greater achievements.

The road to success is never linear. There are times when you will take a few steps forward, only to face setbacks that feel like you're moving backwards. But that's where your true character as an entrepreneur is tested. Do you give up when things get tough, or do you pick yourself up, learn from your mistakes, and continue moving forward?

The ability to learn from failure is one of the most important traits of successful entrepreneurs. It is not the failure that defines you; it is how you respond to it. Every failure, every setback, is an opportunity to improve, to innovate, and to refine your business strategies.

Perseverance: The True Test of an Entrepreneur

The journey of entrepreneurship is not for the faint-hearted. It's not about starting a business and expecting immediate success. It's about building something over time, facing challenges head-on, and never losing sight of your long-term goals. The world of business is constantly changing, and those who are willing to evolve with it are the ones who will thrive.

As you build your business, remember that success requires more than just strategy and hard work. It requires the ability to remain patient, to adapt, and to persevere in the face of adversity. The most successful entrepreneurs are the ones who never give up, who continue learning, and who keep moving forward—no matter the setbacks they face.

The Key to Long-Term Success

The journey of business is long and challenging, but it is also incredibly rewarding. The key to lasting success lies in humility, adaptability, and perseverance. Ego has no place in a successful business. It is not about proving that you're the best; it's about continuously improving, learning, and growing. Those who keep moving forward, who learn from their mistakes, and who embrace change are the ones who will thrive.

Remember, business is bigger than ego. It's about vision, adaptability, and the willingness to do whatever it takes to achieve long-term success. If you can stay grounded, continue to evolve, and persist through challenges, you will find that success is within your reach.

Avoid the Temptation of Politics

Ahmednagar district is widely known as a dairy hub, supplying both pure and adulterated milk across the state. Many politicians in this district have successfully built their businesses around milk collection, processing, and distribution. Some flourished, while others failed. However, what is more striking is how many successful dairy entrepreneurs ruined themselves after stepping into politics. I have seen countless examples of this over the years, and even though I won't name them, their stories serve as important lessons.

In one village, there was a businessman who ran a well-organized milk collection network, supplying milk regularly to the district cooperative dairy. Several others in the area were engaged in similar businesses, and over time, they formed a group of ten people. These were educated men who understood the complexities of the business. In the early 2000s, they decided to establish a dairy collective. For nearly a decade, the business thrived. They expanded their operations, brought in more dairy farmers, and strengthened their reputation. Their influence reached the local political landscape, and soon, they became an important force in Zilla Parishad and Panchayat Samiti elections.

They had built this success through unity, with a shared mindset and a strong sense of cooperation. But with time, ambition got the better of them. When one of them successfully won a local election, the others also felt the urge to enter politics. What began as an entrepreneurial venture gradually turned into a political battleground. Instead of focusing on business growth, they started focusing on their personal influence and political standing. They spent more time attending meetings with influential politicians than running their dairy business.

As they got more involved in politics, they began competing against each other. Their once-close business ties were now strained by rivalry over who had better political connections. The local politicians, sensing their growing influence, saw them as potential threats. To prevent them from becoming too powerful, these politicians deliberately fuelled conflicts within the group. The dairy collective that had once been a model of unity and success slowly crumbled under the weight of ego and political manoeuvring. By 2015, the entire business had collapsed. The members were too preoccupied with their political ambitions, and the dairy they had worked so hard to build was left in shambles.

Even today, people in Ahmednagar talk about the rise and fall of this group. Their story serves as a reminder that success in business does not automatically translate to success in politics. Many talented entrepreneurs have lost everything by assuming that their business acumen would make them good politicians. Politics is a different game, one that requires a different mindset, and not every businessman is suited for it.

This is why entrepreneurs must remain focused on their businesses. The primary goal should be to run an efficient and sustainable enterprise. Getting distracted by political ambitions often leads to unnecessary struggles that could have been avoided.

That being said, it does not mean that businessmen should never be involved in politics. There are a few examples of individuals who have successfully balanced both, such as Nitin Gadkari. He has earned recognition as both a successful entrepreneur and an efficient minister. The key to his success has been his ability to stay focused. He has never let politics divert him from his principles, whether in business or governance.

The Tata Group presents another example. Even Naval Tata, a prominent figure in the company's history, once attempted to enter politics in 1971. However, after failing, no other member of the Tata family pursued a political career again. They understood that their strength lay in business, and they never let political ambitions distract them.

Dhirubhai Ambani and Gautam Adani have followed a similar path. While they undoubtedly maintain strong relationships with political figures, they have never actively engaged in politics themselves. They know that politics and business require different approaches, and trying to do both can be detrimental.

The same is true for business families in Maharashtra. The Kirloskars, Wadias, Birlas, Bajajs, and Shirkes have all deliberately stayed away from direct political involvement. They could have easily secured positions in government or contested elections, but they chose to focus on their industries instead. Their success today is a testament to that decision.

Despite these lessons, it is common to see young businessmen get carried away by their financial success. The moment they establish a moderately profitable business; they start seeking political recognition. They aspire to become members of cooperative societies, contest for the position of sarpanch, or get close to influential politicians. For them, success is measured not just in financial terms but in political validation.

This obsession with political recognition has become a dangerous trend, particularly in Ahmednagar and Marathwada. Today, many people believe that a wedding or a funeral is incomplete unless a politician is present. Entrepreneurs who should be focusing on business expansion are instead fixated on getting photographed with political leaders.

The harsh reality is that politicians do not determine the success of a business—customers do. Yet, many fail to realize this simple truth.

I do not say this as an outsider. Even I have been drawn into politics at times. There was a phase when I welcomed political figures to my personal events and enjoyed the attention that came with their presence. At one point, I even contested a village-level election and attempted to become a cooperative society member. I also worked in political campaign management, believing it would be a valuable experience. But through these encounters, I gained insights into the risks of mixing business with politics.

That is why I decided to share this perspective. This book does not follow a structured beginning or end—just like life and business, it is a continuous journey of learning and adapting.

If there is one lesson to take from this discussion, it is this: entrepreneurs should focus on building and expanding their businesses. Politics can be tempting, but it is often a distraction. Chasing political validation while neglecting business growth is a mistake that has cost many talented individuals their success.

If an entrepreneur chooses to enter politics, they must do so strategically, ensuring that it does not jeopardize their business. At the end of the day, business thrives on satisfied customers, not political affiliations.

CHAPTER FIVE

The Wisdom of Humility and Rationality in Entrepreneurship

One of the most striking traits common among successful entrepreneurs is their ability to engage in meaningful communication, listen attentively, and, most importantly, take rational stances based on careful observation. These qualities, though often underestimated, are vital for carving out a lasting place in the competitive world of business. Entrepreneurs who possess the wisdom of humility and rationality are the ones who make thoughtful decisions, build strong relationships, and ensure the long-term success of their businesses.

The Influence of Community Values on Entrepreneurial Success

In India, many of the most successful businesspeople come from communities such as the Parsis, Jains, Gujaratis, Sindhis, and even Brahmins. These communities have long been associated with commerce and trade, with families passing down entrepreneurial skills through generations. However, what sets these entrepreneurs apart isn't just their business acumen; it's the strong cultural values that are deeply ingrained in them. From small shopkeepers to owners of large businesses, these entrepreneurs exhibit a certain decorum and a humble attitude when interacting with others. This humble approach is not just a matter of politeness—it is a manifestation of the values their families and communities have instilled in them.

Humility and rationality are crucial in business. Entrepreneurs who have cultivated these qualities from their upbringing often possess an innate ability to maintain respectful and professional relationships. They understand that their business exists because of their customers, and this mutual respect is what enables them to build lasting relationships and grow sustainably. Even when they reach success, these entrepreneurs tend to remain grounded, aware that their journey is not just about individual achievement but also about contributing to the broader community.

The Role of Rationality in Ensuring Long-Term Success

Rationality plays a central role in the success of these businesses. Many successful family-run businesses maintain professionalism, respect, and continuity—values that have been ingrained over generations. These businesses tend to endure because they are not driven by short-term goals or egos but by the rational understanding that lasting success requires patience, consistency, and a commitment to ethical practices. For example, businesses that treat employees, customers, and suppliers with respect, and operate with a sense of fairness, are more likely to build trust and loyalty over time.

One of the primary reasons why these family businesses have an edge is that they focus on long-term relationships and sustainability rather than just profit. By valuing rationality and mutual respect, these entrepreneurs make decisions that ensure the future of the business, even if it means forgoing immediate rewards for long-term benefits.

The Pitfalls of Arrogance in New Entrepreneurs

On the other hand, new entrepreneurs—especially those from backgrounds where business traditions are less deeply rooted—often struggle to maintain this level of humility and rationality. The excitement of early success can cloud their judgment and give rise to an inflated sense of self-importance. When these entrepreneurs begin to taste success, it's easy for them to develop a feeling of superiority over others, believing that they have accomplished something extraordinary and that the world owes them.

This sense of pride can quickly transform into arrogance, which can have a devastating impact on their businesses. Arrogance can lead to poor decision-making, such as neglecting the needs and concerns of customers, treating employees unfairly, or refusing to listen to feedback. More importantly, it can damage relationships with clients, partners, and stakeholders, eroding the foundation of trust and respect that is crucial for business growth.

The Damage Caused by Ego

Ego-driven behaviour often leads to an unsustainable business model. For example, entrepreneurs who believe their success is a favour to the world may treat their customers as if they are indebted to them. They might enter their stores or offices with an air of superiority, expecting customers to be grateful simply for the privilege of buying from them. This kind of attitude can alienate customers, leaving them feeling undervalued and unappreciated.

This sense of entitlement not only tarnishes the entrepreneur's reputation but also creates a toxic work environment, one where employees feel demotivated and disengaged. When entrepreneurs prioritize their ego over the rational principles of customer service, employee well-being, and product quality, the business begins to unravel. What initially appeared to be a thriving business may soon find itself in a downward spiral, struggling to maintain its foothold in the market.

The Importance of Rational Decision-Making

To avoid falling into the trap of arrogance, entrepreneurs must focus on rational decision-making. Rationality involves recognizing that success does not come from ego, but from a clear understanding of the market, the needs of customers, and the strengths and weaknesses of one's own business. Successful entrepreneurs are those who are willing to listen to feedback, adapt to changes, and make informed decisions that are grounded in reality, not pride.

By maintaining a rational perspective, entrepreneurs can better navigate challenges, build sustainable business models, and create a positive reputation that attracts loyal customers and employees. It's also essential to recognize that success is a continuous process—one that requires ongoing learning, humility, and a willingness to grow.

The Bottom Line: Humility and Rationality as Pillars of Success

Ultimately, the wisdom of humility and rationality is what separates successful entrepreneurs from those who falter. Humility allows entrepreneurs to remain grounded, to recognize that their success is not solely the result of their own efforts, but of the support and trust of their customers, employees, and communities. Rationality helps them make thoughtful, data-driven decisions that support long-term growth and sustainability.

For entrepreneurs looking to build lasting businesses, focusing on these two qualities is essential. By staying humble and rational, entrepreneurs can foster relationships based on respect and trust, make wise decisions that propel their businesses forward, and avoid the pitfalls of ego that can derail their success.

Building a Sustainable Business with Humility and Rationality

Success in entrepreneurship is not about flaunting one's achievements or asserting dominance in the marketplace. It's about fostering trust, maintaining professionalism, and making decisions based on rational analysis rather than ego-driven impulses. Entrepreneurs who understand the value of humility and rationality are better equipped to navigate the ups and downs of the business world and create sustainable, thriving enterprises. These qualities, nurtured through community values and family upbringing, are the pillars upon which long- term success is built.

The Importance of Listening and Understanding the Customer

In any business—be it retail, hospitality, or services—the customer is the heart of the operation. Without them, there would be no reason for the business to exist. However, in today's fast-paced world, particularly with the rise of start-ups and digital entrepreneurs, many businesses overlook the fundamental principle of truly listening to their customers. It's not enough to simply offer a product or service; businesses must understand their customers' needs, expectations, and underlying concerns to thrive.

Listening to the customer means more than hearing their words. It's about paying attention to their unspoken desires and figuring out how to meet their needs in a way that adds real value. Understanding the customer deeply allows businesses to identify problems and create solutions that resonate with the consumer. This approach ensures that businesses remain relevant, adaptive, and able to offer meaningful experiences to their customers.

Rationality plays a critical role in this process. Entrepreneurs who approach their customers with a rational mindset recognize that business is not about showing off or asserting dominance but about problem-solving. When business owners genuinely seek to meet consumer needs, they foster loyalty and long-term success. Customers are not merely transactions; they are the lifeblood of a business, and satisfying their needs is essential for growth.

The Perils of Ego in Entrepreneurship

An entrepreneur's journey is fraught with obstacles, but one of the greatest challenges comes from within—their own ego. Ego, while a natural human trait, can be a double-edged sword. While it can drive ambition and fuel success, unchecked ego can quickly become destructive. Arrogance, complacency, and overconfidence often arise when the ego is allowed to control decision-making, leading to poor judgment and even failure.

Just as in the animal kingdom, where dominance and hierarchy are established through displays of ego, humans have a similar tendency. Entrepreneurs often feel compelled to display their power, control, or success. However, the key to achieving lasting success is not in flaunting ego, but in managing it effectively. A successful entrepreneur knows when to temper their ego and focus on the work at hand.

The best entrepreneurs recognize that success isn't about grand gestures or ostentatious displays of wealth. True success comes from consistency, dedication, and the ability to remain humble even in the face of achievement. Humility builds trust, and trust fosters long-term relationships with customers, clients, and employees. Over time, humility enhances the entrepreneur's reputation, ensuring that their business remains respected and their clients continue to return.

The Dangers of Vanity in the Age of Social Media

In today's digital age, vanity and the desire to be seen are more pronounced than ever. Social media platforms like Instagram, LinkedIn, and Twitter have made it easy to project a false image of success. Many young entrepreneurs, in particular, fall into the trap of focusing on outward appearances rather than substance. The desire to be seen as successful often leads to the pursuit of likes, followers, and endorsements, sometimes at the expense of the actual work needed to build a sustainable business.

The "fake it till you make it" mentality, popularized on social media, can be tempting. While it may generate short-term attention, it rarely leads to lasting success. The focus on outward displays of success, such as flashy posts or extravagant lifestyles, diverts attention from the core of the business—the product or service that delivers real value to customers. Businesses that focus on superficial appearances risk losing sight of the fundamentals that lead to long-term growth.

In contrast, entrepreneurs like Steve Jobs and Warren Buffet found success not through flaunting their wealth but by focusing on their core values. Jobs remained deeply focused on innovation, constantly pushing the boundaries of technology to improve user experiences. Buffet, on the other hand, built his empire by consistently applying value investing principles. Both men understood that true success in business is built on consistent hard work, credibility, and a commitment to adding value—not on outward displays of wealth or status.

The True Measure of Success

Ultimately, the measure of success in business is not about how many likes or followers you accumulate, but about the real impact you have on your customers and the market. A successful entrepreneur is someone who builds a business that provides value, solves problems, and improves lives. It's about creating lasting relationships with customers, employees, and partners, and staying focused on the bigger picture.

The wisdom of entrepreneurs like Steve Jobs and Warren Buffet highlights the importance of focusing on the fundamentals—innovation, value, and consistency—rather than the distractions of vanity and ego. Business owners who understand this principle will always be better positioned for long-term success.

Humility vs. Arrogance in Business Practice

Therefore, the true path to success in business does not lie in arrogance, showmanship, or a bloated sense of self-importance. Rather, it is found in the qualities of humility, rationality, and a dedication to providing real value. The most successful entrepreneurs are those who understand that their role is not to place themselves above others, but to offer meaningful solutions to the problems their customers face. They approach their businesses with respect for the customer and a commitment to excellence in both the products and services they provide.

While ego is a natural aspect of human nature, in business, it must be managed with care. Entrepreneurs who are able to recognize when their ego is becoming a hindrance to growth are the ones who endure and thrive in the long run. Humility is not about diminishing one's achievements but about understanding that success comes from a continuous effort to learn, adapt, and grow. By focusing on delivering value rather than showcasing one's accomplishments, entrepreneurs can create a lasting and meaningful impact.

In the competitive world of business, the ability to listen, understand, and act with rationality will always outweigh the temptation to flaunt one's success. Business is not about seeking admiration or approval, but about building something substantial—something that can endure and continue to serve customers for years to come. Humility, when paired with a focus on providing value, creates a business legacy that stands the test of time.

Treat Everyone with Respect, and You Will Earn Respect in Return

Currently, my business involves supplying goods at the government level. In simple terms, I am a government contractor. The moment people hear the word "contractor," a certain image flashes in their minds—a man who flaunts his wealth, has strong political connections, and carries an air of arrogance. Whether these traits are strengths or weaknesses, I cannot say for sure.

What I do know is that my company has grown steadily because we focus on delivering quality products and services. At the same time, I see others in the same field growing at an even faster pace because they understand the deeper tricks of the trade. Perhaps our progress has been slower because we refuse to adopt certain shortcuts. This is true in every business. Watching others succeed should not make us feel insecure, nor should achieving success make us look down upon society. We consciously remind ourselves to remain grounded, valuing the time and efforts of others just as we value our own.

This brings me to an important realization—respecting people's time and money is the key to a successful business relationship.

The Value of Time in Business

In 2022, we secured a significant order for solar equipment. To procure the required materials, a friend suggested visiting a well-known dealer in Ahmednagar. The dealer asked us to meet him at 2:00 PM at his warehouse. Understanding the importance of punctuality in business, we arrived well before time, expecting a professional interaction.

However, the dealer was nowhere to be seen. Assuming a slight delay, we decided to wait. His staff was lounging around, chatting, and enjoying their lunch, completely ignoring us. By 3:30 PM, there was still no sign of him. Repeated calls to his phone went unanswered—it was switched off. Finally, at 4:00 PM, we gave up and left, heading to a nearby restaurant to grab a meal before returning home.

Later in the evening, my friend called with an explanation. The dealer had gone upstairs for his routine afternoon nap. He had asked us to arrive at 2:00 PM, knowing well that he would be unavailable by 2:30. He had simply followed his daily habit of turning off his phone and taking a nap, disregarding the commitment he had made.

By then, we had already decided to look elsewhere. The next morning, I reached out to a much larger agency in Ahmednagar, one that was far more professional. When we met, they took the time to understand our order, assessed our financial capability, and appreciated our structured approach. Without unnecessary delays, they provided us with material worth over a crore, requiring only a modest advance payment of ₹50,000.

Our business relationship with them continues to flourish. Despite handling transactions worth hundreds of crores, they have never once belittled us for being a smaller vendor.

Months later, the original dealer who had ignored us came to our office, hoping to secure business from us. We welcomed him politely, offered him tea, but ultimately declined his offer. The experience had taught us a valuable lesson—anyone who does not respect another's time and efforts is not worth working with.

Respect is the Foundation of Business

One of my business mentors, Dnyandev Bhosale, has always emphasized the importance of respect. Even on his busiest days, he takes the time to greet people courteously, ensuring that no customer or vendor ever feels ignored. His approach has always resonated with me.

After all, don't we all prefer dealing with polite and well-mannered shopkeepers or managers? The moment we feel valued, we are more inclined to continue doing business with someone. Respect is a universal need—just as we seek respect, others expect the same from us. This is not just a principle for business; it is a principle for life.

Business is Practicality, Not Just Social Sentiment

We often hear statements like, "I want to start a business to serve society," or "My business will uplift the underprivileged." Such words sound noble in public speeches, podcasts, and social media posts. However, the reality of running a business is quite different.

The truth is, we do not start businesses out of charity. We do it to generate profit. Profit is what allows us to create financial and social stability, and only then do we gain the ability to help others.

Years ago, I learned this lesson the hard way. Coming from a background where I admired socialist ideals, I initially believed that profit should be secondary and that businesses should focus on uplifting farmers and labourers. With this mindset, I ventured into the business of selling neem cake fertilizer, aiming to provide farmers with a high-quality product at a fair price.

Neem cake is an excellent natural fertilizer, but it is also expensive. The cheaper versions available in the market are often adulterated, finely ground, and stripped of oil content. I, however, supplied genuine neem cake, which contained all its natural nutrients. Unfortunately, because of its unprocessed nature, some batches contained small stone particles, which was unavoidable.

Initially, farmers appreciated the quality, but rumours soon spread that I was intentionally adding stones to increase weight. As a result, some refused to pay, leading to financial losses.

Ironically, after my business shut down, many of those same farmers admitted that my product had been superior and encouraged me to restart. By then, however, I had learned my lesson.

A business must be sustainable, not charitable. If we reduce our profit margins too much in an attempt to help others, we will ultimately be unable to sustain our business.

A Business Must Be Both Ethical and Profitable

Failure has a way of teaching lessons that no book can. Through my experiences, I have come to understand that a successful business must strike a balance between quality, ethics, and profitability.

A product or service should be of the highest quality. Pricing should be fair but should never be reduced so much that it harms the business. Without profitability, survival is impossible, and if the business collapses, it benefits no one—not the entrepreneur, not the employees, and not the society.

People do not need charity; they need reliable, fair, and sustainable business solutions. A practical business mindset is what prevents exploitation, builds long-term financial strength, and allows genuine contributions to society.

At the same time, practicality does not mean greed. Ethical business practices must remain at the core of everything. Those who only think about social service without considering financial sustainability will fail. Those who are driven only by profit will make money but will never earn respect. The right approach is a balance—ensuring value for customers, maintaining healthy profits, and aiming for long-term success.

At the end of the day, business should give us a sense of fulfillment. If we cannot sleep peacefully at night despite having wealth, what is the point? If our success is built on deception, it will not last. Real success is not just about making money—it is about doing business in a way that is ethical, smart, and sustainable.

CHAPTER SIX

"Beyond Fear, there is Victory!"

The phrase "Fear is the path to victory" resonates deeply in the real world of entrepreneurship. This message is echoed in the advertisements of brands like Mountain Dew, which emphasize the importance of confronting and overcoming fear in order to achieve success. Every decision we make, every new step we take, is accompanied by uncertainties and risks. At such junctures, we must take calculated risks, deciding to move forward despite the unknown. The decision often boils down to two choices: one is to remain passive, avoiding action due to fear of consequences, while the other is to face the fear head-on, trusting that the results will follow.

In both life and business, we are continually faced with fear and uncertainty. Moving forward, despite the fear, is often the best option. Whether in personal life or in entrepreneurship, the key to success lies in constantly overcoming fears.

Facing Fear in Business

Starting a business is never easy; it comes with numerous challenges, problems, and a sense of fear. Many young people, especially young women, may assume that starting a business requires immense courage. While this assumption holds some truth, it is also important to recognize that in business, success is never guaranteed. The odds of success and failure rarely balance out, and this dynamic exists not only in India but across the world. However, in countries like India, the probability of success is lower, not necessarily because of a lack of potential, but because opportunities are fewer and the competition is fierce.

The competition for success doesn't just exist in business; it's present in everyday jobs as employees compete for promotions and recognition. In India, this competition has become the foundation of the system. In such a competitive environment, the mantra "Beyond fear, there is victory" becomes crucial. Victory, whether in business or life, lies on the other side of fear.

The Role of Fear in Business Success

Fear, in business, takes many forms. It's not just the entrepreneur who fears failure but also their friends, family, and competitors. The fear of failure, fear of loss, fear of missed opportunities, and even the fear of competitors surpassing you all play a part. Yet, ironically, it is this fear that often pushes entrepreneurs to move forward. Fear, when understood and confronted, can transform into an opportunity.

Fear, like failure, is an integral part of the journey to success. It isn't an obstacle but an essential step toward progress. Many successful entrepreneurs have faced failure early in their careers, but they didn't let those failures define them. Instead, they learned from their mistakes and kept pushing forward. Today, they are recognized as leaders in their industries.

Failure is not an endpoint but a beginning—a new opportunity for growth. The saying "Failure is the first step to success" holds true. If we allow fear of failure to stop us, we can never reach victory. The true key to success is not avoiding failure, but learning from it and continuing to move forward with renewed strength and purpose.

Managing Fear to Unlock Opportunities

Fear is a natural part of the human experience, and it must be managed properly to prevent it from dominating our thoughts and actions. If fear is left unchecked, it can lead to stagnation and missed opportunities. However, acknowledging and addressing fear can pave the way for growth, self-discovery, and, ultimately, success. The key lies in managing this fear, not letting it control us, and ensuring it doesn't trap us in negative thinking patterns that block progress.

Those who claim to fear nothing are often not the best sources of guidance, as they may overlook the importance of managing fear in a healthy way. Real success isn't about eliminating fear; it's about facing it and making bold decisions in spite of it. Overcoming fear and moving forward, despite the uncertainty, is what leads to long-term success. To truly unlock opportunities, we must be willing to take risks, knowing that failure to confront fear means missing out on growth and success.

Fear and Its Impact on Self-Confidence

One of the most significant impacts of fear is that it can erode self-confidence. Fear creates a mindset that undermines our belief in ourselves, making us feel small or incapable. However, when we face our fears head-on, we realize that the fear was often irrational, and in doing so, our confidence grows.

"Fear leads to victory" isn't just about overcoming fear and achieving success; it's about the courage, self-confidence, and resilience that emerge from facing our fears. Each time we confront a problem or a challenging situation, we discover strengths we didn't know we had. In these moments, we learn our true potential, which builds an inner confidence that becomes a powerful asset when facing future obstacles.

This newfound confidence is not a fleeting emotion but a long-lasting change in how we approach life. It gives us the courage to take on bigger challenges and keep pushing forward, knowing that even if we fail, we have the strength to try again and persevere.

New Challenges and Overcoming Fear

Every step we take in life, whether in business or personal endeavours, brings new challenges. Initially, these challenges might seem overwhelming or frightening. The unknown always carries a degree of fear. But overcoming these challenges is what transforms fear into victory. It is only by embracing fear and learning to navigate it that we unlock our true potential and the doors to success.

The true measure of success lies not in avoiding fear or escaping challenges, but in confronting and overcoming them. Each challenge is an opportunity for growth and a stepping stone toward a greater achievement. By facing fear and embracing the challenges that life presents, we open ourselves up to new opportunities, confidence, and, ultimately, victory.

Success is not about being fearless; it's about understanding that fear is a part of the journey and that we can rise above it. Through fear, we discover courage. Through courage, we discover success. The mantra "Fear leads to victory" becomes real when we not only confront our fears but use them as stepping stones to reach our goals.

Success Lies Beyond Fear and Defeat

Entrepreneurship is defined by the ability to face fear head-on, accept defeat when it happens, and keep moving forward despite challenges. The principle "Fear leads to victory" speaks to the necessity of confronting fear to unlock opportunities, but "Beyond defeat, there is victory" is just as essential in the entrepreneurial journey. Entrepreneurs who are willing to embrace failure, learn from it, and persist are the ones who ultimately succeed.

Victory, in this sense, is not a singular, final achievement but a continuous journey. Overcoming fear, accepting failure, and turning these experiences into lessons is what truly defines success in business. Every entrepreneur has faced moments of doubt, fear, and failure. But by transforming those experiences into opportunities for growth, they set the stage for greater accomplishments.

The True Path to Success

Business success is not just about reaching a final destination, but about cultivating the resilience to overcome fear, the courage to learn from mistakes, and the wisdom to recognize that each setback is a stepping stone toward something greater. The mantra "Beyond fear, there is victory" encapsulates this journey. Success in business comes not from avoiding challenges but from facing them head-on, learning from failures, and pushing forward despite them.

Every successful entrepreneur has encountered obstacles, experienced fear, and faced defeat. What sets them apart is their ability to rise above those experiences, to keep moving forward, and to view failure as part of the path to success. "Beyond defeat, there is victory" because each time we face a setback or challenge, we learn something valuable that brings us closer to achieving our ultimate goal.

Success—both in business and in life—is built on courage, perseverance, and the relentless pursuit of one's dreams. So, whether you're just starting out or scaling your business, remember: fear is not your enemy. It is the gateway to your victory.

Victory and Defeat: A Never-Ending Cycle

In business, as in life, success and failure come in cycles. No matter how skilled, experienced, or prepared a person is, they will inevitably face ups and downs. Just as roads have steep climbs and sharp descents, every business journey has its own unpredictable turns. No entrepreneur, no matter how powerful, has escaped these fluctuations—nor will anyone in the future.

A perfect example of this cycle of rise and fall is the Tata Group. When Jamshedji Tata founded the Tata Iron and Steel Company (TISCO) in 1907, his vision was to build a strong steel industry in India. However, the early years were filled with financial struggles and technological setbacks. The British administration, which controlled India at the time, created multiple obstacles. Yet, history took an unexpected turn. During World War II, the same British government that once made things difficult for Tata now relied on their steel supply for military production. This became the company's breakthrough moment, strengthening its foundation and ensuring its long-term success.

Another chapter in Tata's journey highlights the unpredictable nature of business. In 1998, Tata Motors launched India's first fully indigenous car, the Indica. However, the market did not respond favourably. The technology seemed outdated, and customers were not impressed with the overall quality. The project, which had been a dream for the company, quickly turned into a commercial failure. It was a major setback, and many would have expected Tata to abandon the idea of car manufacturing. But instead of quitting, the company took the feedback seriously, made improvements, and worked on better models. The Nano project faced a similar fate. Though it was introduced as the world's most affordable car, it struggled with branding issues, and customers did not embrace it as expected. However, the setbacks did not deter the company. They continued to innovate, refine their strategies, and learn from their mistakes. Today, Tata Motors stands as a globally respected automobile manufacturer, proving that persistence and adaptability transform failures into success.

The Tata Group's story serves as a reminder that failure is not the end. It is simply a phase that tests resilience and the willingness to improve. Every entrepreneur, whether big or small, will face struggles. But those who accept challenges, adapt, and continue to move forward will ultimately emerge stronger. Business success is never permanent, nor is failure. What matters is the ability to evolve, to understand the lessons hidden within each setback, and to use them as stepping stones toward a stronger future.

The Key to Progress: Professional Skills

Skill development, often referred to as "Skill India," has become one of the pivotal mantras for the vision of New India. This emphasis on skilling is not just a modern trend but a necessary evolution, especially given the historical backdrop of our education system. In many ways, the Indian education model has functioned more like a factory assembly line, churning out a generation of youth who possess theoretical knowledge yet lack practical expertise. These young individuals, trained to memorize and repeat information, often find themselves at a disadvantage when they step into the real world, which values tangible skills and critical thinking.

The reality of this situation has become increasingly evident over the years. We witnessed a wave of youth pursuing D.Ed. and B.Ed. degrees, flooding every corner of the nation, from bustling cities to remote villages. Shortly after, this wave was overshadowed by a surge of engineering graduates, followed by a mass influx of students from IT, pharma, MBA programs, and even graduates in arts, commerce, or science from various institutions. This overwhelming supply of degree-holding job seekers has diluted the value of conventional academic qualifications, highlighting a fundamental gap in our approach to education.

I, too, was swept away in this tide of educational expectations. Influenced by family friends and societal norms, I ended up in the science stream. My academic journey was anything but smooth—I struggled, barely managing to pass my 12th-grade exams. My first year of B.Sc. proved to be a breaking point when I failed three subjects. It was a harsh realization of my limitations but also a moment of awakening. During this difficult period, I contemplated preparing for MPSC (Maharashtra Public Service Commission) and UPSC (Union Public Service Commission) exams, driven more by societal pressure than personal ambition. Yet, I found myself grappling with the uncertainty of a future in which I had no clear purpose.

That same year in Nashik, a turning point arrived through Sunita Sudrik, who introduced me to Yashwantrao Chavan Open University. Her words made me question why I was enduring the struggle of pursuing a science degree that I didn't even enjoy. It became clear that my path lay elsewhere, and I bid farewell to B.Sc., shifting to the arts stream. This change ignited my curiosity, sparking an interest in extracurricular reading and the endless resources provided by Google. For the first time, I truly grasped the importance of acquiring practical skills. My fear of venturing into the world of work dissipated, and I embraced opportunities like participating in the employment guarantee scheme, where I even earned government wheat. This experience of stepping outside the bounds of academic pressure gave me a new perspective on the value of hands-on work.

The key lesson from my story is not just about my journey but the broader realization that recognizing the importance of skills early on is crucial. We must break free from the outdated mindset that views manual labour or skill-based work as something to be ashamed of. The truth is, understanding the necessity of learning the right skills at the right age—and having the courage to pursue them—can transform one's life. While it's not mandatory to master any specific skill, the willingness to develop abilities relevant to the changing world is essential. Unfortunately, our Indian education system has not kept up with this need, remaining rooted in methods that prepare students more for clerical roles than for a world demanding innovation and adaptability.

The systemic problem lies in an education model that emphasizes memorization over questioning, where students are taught to regurgitate answers rather than engage in critical thinking. As a result, many of us who have been shaped by this system are ill-equipped to challenge political or social injustices, often bowing our heads in silent submission. To advance as a nation, both socially and economically, we need a generation that isn't afraid to question the status quo, to harness their natural curiosity, and to learn how to apply knowledge practically.

It is essential to understand that those who have a clear vision of what they want in life—and, equally importantly, what they want to avoid—are the ones who eventually find success. In today's world, the combination of knowledge and practical skills is far more valuable than information alone. It's crucial to prepare for this reality and to start early. By the age of

20, while still in school, students have numerous opportunities to explore. It's important to observe and understand your surroundings, evaluate your physical and mental strengths, and align them with the resources and support you receive from your family. Earn your family's trust by demonstrating sincerity and commitment to your goals. Seek out people who have established themselves in your field of interest, as well as those who have experienced failure. Learn from their journeys, gather insights, and use this knowledge to cultivate the skills you need.

Communication Skills: The Foundation of Success

One of the most critical skills to acquire is effective communication. In Marathi, there's a saying: "The talkative sell wheat, but the silent one can't even sell barley." This simple proverb underscores the necessity of being articulate and engaging. Yet, communication is not about speaking for the sake of speaking. In the worlds of politics and religion, there are countless examples of individuals who have gained popularity by making exaggerated or nonsensical statements. However, the business world operates differently. In professional and social settings, reckless or thoughtless communication can be detrimental.

True communication is a two-way street. It's not just about expressing your thoughts but also about listening and understanding others. Listening is a vital part of the communication process. Our guide, the late M.B. Shinde sir, always emphasized, "Marketing is not a big game; marketing is about communicating properly." His simple yet profound definition of marketing remains etched in my mind. In the same vein, successful communication in business requires clarity, respect, and the ability to convey your message effectively.

Good communication involves building trust, avoiding misunderstandings, and connecting with people on a deeper level. Whether speaking or writing, your message must be clear and easily comprehensible. To achieve this, you must learn to actively listen, engage in meaningful conversations, and present your ideas logically and persuasively. Only then can you achieve true success in any business endeavour.

Leadership Skills

Chatrapati Shivaji Maharaj stands as a timeless source of inspiration to people across Maharashtra and beyond. His remarkable leadership earned him unwavering respect and loyalty from his commanders and followers, and it wasn't merely by chance. The legacy he left behind serves as a testament to the transformative power of genuine leadership. Leaders who leave a lasting impact, whether in the realms of politics, business, or society, are distinguished by their ability to inspire and guide rather than simply issue commands. Leadership is far more complex than directing people or pushing them to complete tasks; it involves understanding the struggles and challenges faced by those you lead and providing them with the guidance they need.

A strong leader recognizes that success does not come from doing all the work themselves. Instead, they empower and motivate their team, fostering a cooperative and collaborative environment. This approach not only builds trust but also enhances the efficiency and effectiveness of the entire group. Importantly, leadership skills do not come pre-packaged at birth. These abilities must be cultivated and honed over time through a continuous process of learning, observing, reflecting, and contemplating. Engaging with insightful literature, analysing leadership models, and thoughtfully considering various situations all contribute to the development of these vital skills. By starting young, aspiring leaders can better prepare themselves to face life's challenges and inspire others.

Problem-Solving Skills

Life, in its simplest definition, is a series of problems and their complexities. No one is immune to challenges, whether in personal life or professional endeavours. The key, however, lies in how one chooses to confront and handle these inevitable obstacles. Problems are not an indication of failure or defeat; rather, they are opportunities wrapped in challenges. Accepting this reality is crucial, especially for those who aspire to thrive in the business world. Problems will continue to arise, but that should never deter anyone from pursuing their goals. It is through engaging with difficulties, finding solutions, and ultimately overcoming them that one experiences the true joy and satisfaction of the practical world.

Mastering the art of problem-solving is an essential skill that distinguishes successful individuals. It begins with a mindset shift: viewing problems not as barriers but as opportunities to learn and grow. When obstacles present themselves, the natural instinct may be to take shortcuts or avoid them altogether, but genuine success comes from tackling these issues head-on. Calm and composed thinking are critical. By maintaining a clear and focused mind, you can generate multiple potential solutions and choose the best one. Developing strong analytical and creative thinking abilities enables you to navigate through challenges with greater ease and effectiveness. It's all about preparedness and the mental resilience to handle any situation that arises.

Time Management

Time is the most equitable resource in existence. Each of us is granted the same 24 hours in a day and 365 days in a year. Nature has ensured that time is distributed evenly among all, regardless of status or wealth. However, the difference between success and failure often lies in how we use this finite resource. Effective time management is a skill that plays a crucial role in achieving professional and personal success. It's common to hear people complain, "I don't have time," or "I'm too busy," particularly when they fail to meet obligations or serve their customers well. In reality, these complaints are often rooted in a lack of proper time management.

Managing time is about more than simply allocating hours to tasks; it involves prioritizing and understanding which activities deserve more focus and which can be completed more quickly. Those who lack this skill frequently find themselves overwhelmed, leading to the familiar refrain, "I don't have time." Even the most talented individuals can face setbacks in business if they fail to manage their time effectively. In India, a peculiar superstition persists that those who are punctual are either foolish or overly clever. This cultural perception adds another layer of challenge for individuals striving to manage their time well.

However, time management doesn't require a rigid, inflexible schedule. Instead, it involves developing a disciplined yet adaptable approach to planning. Having a sense of responsibility toward punctuality and task completion is crucial. By finishing tasks on time and adhering to well-thought-out plans, one can significantly boost productivity and efficiency. Young people, in particular, should adopt this habit early, focusing on important tasks and making the most of every moment. Cultivating strong time management skills can lay the foundation for a successful and well-organized future.

Teamwork

Teamwork is an essential component of success, and the stories of many great leaders and successful figures illustrate this truth. Take, for example, the legendary actor Dada Kondke, who often declared, "Ekta jeev sadashiv" (a single life is all-powerful). While his hard work and talent played significant roles in his achievements, he also owed much to the contributions of the people around him. History is full of examples of rulers and kings who, despite their immense bravery and capabilities, met with failure because they neglected the value of teamwork. On the other hand, Chatrapati Shivaji Maharaj, who prioritized collective effort and genuinely cared for the well-being of his people, became a celebrated figure who changed the course of history.

Emperor Akbar's successful expansion of his empire similarly relied on his ability to unify and collaborate with diverse groups of people. In the modern business world, companies like the Tata Group have thrived by recognizing the unique talents of each team member and creating an environment that allows these skills to flourish. Conversely, ignoring teamwork can lead to disastrous outcomes, as evidenced by the fall of Anil Ambani's empire, which suffered from an overemphasis on grand slogans like "Kar lo duniya mutthi mein" (Conquer the world) and a lack of cohesive collaboration.

The reality is that no one can achieve significant success in business or any field without the support of a strong team. Running a small tea stall might allow for a one-person operation, but even that requires dedication and effort. In a professional business setting, teamwork is indispensable. A good businessman understands the importance of harnessing the collective strengths of their team members. Every individual in a team brings unique skills to the table, and utilizing these diverse abilities in a coordinated manner can lead to exceptional outcomes. Success comes from the ability to work well with others, recognize their potential, and inspire them to give their best.

Creativity

Running a business is far from a straightforward task. It demands a keen awareness of market needs and a deep understanding of your own abilities to determine which business ventures you should pursue. A central pillar in this process is creativity—the ability to generate fresh, novel ideas, think outside traditional frameworks, and bring innovative approaches to business practices. Creativity is about reimagining possibilities, whether in marketing strategies, product design, customer engagement, or even management techniques. However, there is a fine line between useful creativity and an overabundance of it. When you attempt to take on too many creative endeavours or feel an overwhelming urge to execute every idea by yourself, it can become harmful to your overall progress. The pursuit of creativity should be balanced, and it's important to recognize when you need help. Even if you feel confident that you have all the answers, not every business problem is solvable by sheer inventiveness or with a "do-it-all-yourself" approach. Sometimes, ideas require refinement and collaboration to reach their full potential.

It is perfectly acceptable to have visions, thoughts, or a business plan simmering in your mind. Yet, jumping headfirst into every opportunity without careful planning or input from others can lead to wasteful efforts. Therefore, it is critical to apply your creativity wisely. Engaging in discussions with like-minded individuals, such as other entrepreneurs and collaborators, can lead to more refined and actionable strategies. This is especially relevant when mentoring or guiding young entrepreneurs who may benefit immensely from your experiences. Sharing your creative insights and offering support to others just beginning their entrepreneurial journeys can be fulfilling. Witnessing their growth as they act on your advice adds a layer of satisfaction to your own achievements, making creativity not just about your own success but about building a thriving, collaborative community.

Patience and Perseverance

Reflecting on my personal experiences, there was a time when my creativity knew no bounds, leading me to embark on countless business ventures. Unfortunately, many of these endeavours did not survive, resulting in significant financial losses. These failures, in retrospect, were fuelled by an overconfidence in my ability to transform every idea into a successful enterprise. At that point, I did not fully appreciate the necessity of two fundamental traits: patience and perseverance. Without patience, even the most determined and passionate efforts can fall short. The business world is full of challenges, and success is rarely instantaneous. It's through enduring setbacks and patiently working through obstacles that real progress is made.

Patience is not merely about waiting; it's about maintaining a proactive, positive attitude while waiting for your hard work to pay off. Perseverance, on the other hand, is about the continuous, unwavering commitment to your goals despite the inevitable hurdles. Reflecting on past failures, I realize how a lack of these qualities led to rushed decisions and hasty investments. If I had adopted a more patient, methodical approach, perhaps some of my ventures would have turned out differently. Over time, I have come to appreciate that a "wait and watch" strategy often yields better results than trying to force immediate success. Observing how other leaders and entrepreneurs, who may not have reached their ultimate goals, continue to work with dedication, serves as a constant reminder. Consider political figures like Mulayam Singh Yadav, Pramod Mahajan, L.K. Advani, and Sharad Pawar. Though they may have aspired to be prime ministers and never achieved that specific title, they did not lose their purpose. They kept contributing to their fields, proving that success is about persistence, not just about achieving one major milestone.

The journey to success is not defined solely by the grandeur of your accomplishments. Success is multi-dimensional; it includes not only personal achievements but also the ability to create an atmosphere of positivity and growth for those around you. It's about building a legacy where your efforts inspire and uplift others. If success were simply measured by being the top earner or having the highest turnover, then only a select few would be deemed successful. But true success lies in navigating the highs and lows of life and business with grace and determination. Life, much like business, is full of unexpected turns. It is these very fluctuations—these moments of triumph and failure—that make the experience rich and fulfilling. Therefore, cultivating the strength to keep moving forward, to stay active, and to persevere with a positive outlook is essential. The key lies in being ready to adapt and to put in consistent, patient effort, knowing that perseverance ultimately paves the way for success.

Along with the important points mentioned above, we should also master the following skills:

Skill Utilization

Skill utilization extends far beyond simply learning new skills; it is about knowing how to apply them effectively and appropriately in various situations. At the heart of this concept lies a positive attitude, which is essential for professional and personal growth. A positive attitude does not mean being unrealistically optimistic or assuming that everything will always work out in your favour. Rather, it means maintaining a mindset that is open to exploration and learning. When you approach opportunities or challenges, a willingness to investigate and test possibilities can yield surprising benefits. Even if you are unsure about the outcome, having a proactive and inquisitive attitude will always enrich your understanding and capabilities. Of course, if something genuinely does not seem to be working or aligning with your goals, you are free to step away. However, a positive outlook ensures that you give yourself a fair chance to try, to learn, and to grow before making any final decisions.

The idea of a positive mindset also emphasizes effort over outcome. In any venture—be it starting a business, launching a project, or even pursuing a hobby—the true value lies not in always winning but in giving your best effort. When you engage wholeheartedly, even if things do not turn out as expected, there is a sense of fulfillment in knowing you tried earnestly. This philosophy reduces regret and increases satisfaction, reinforcing the belief that effort is worthwhile, irrespective of the immediate result. Approaching life and business with this understanding prepares you to face uncertainties without the fear of failure overshadowing your willingness to act.

Willingness to Let Go

Life is unpredictable, and outcomes do not always match our expectations. In our personal and professional journeys, it is common to face situations where things do not unfold as we had hoped. This is where the ability to let go becomes an invaluable skill. Often, even the best-laid plans may not yield the desired results. In such moments, holding on stubbornly to a failing course of action can be counterproductive. It takes courage and maturity to step back, reassess the situation, and recognize when it is time to move on. Letting go does not imply giving up easily; rather, it is about being wise enough to understand when persistence is no longer effective.

Before making any drastic decisions, it is important to gather all relevant information, consult with mentors or colleagues, and evaluate whether continuing is truly the best option. If you determine that it is more beneficial to change direction, you should do so without guilt or regret. Walking away from an unfruitful endeavour is not a sign of weakness but a testament to your strategic thinking and adaptability. The key is to balance determination with discernment, making choices that serve your long-term interests while remaining flexible and pragmatic.

Self-Confidence

Self-confidence serves as the cornerstone of any successful endeavour. Believing in yourself, your abilities, and your vision is crucial for navigating the complexities of both business and life. This self-assurance empowers you to make bold decisions, face obstacles with courage, and keep moving forward even when the path seems uncertain. It is the inner belief that gives you the strength to pursue your ambitions despite external doubts or challenges. However, while self-confidence is essential, it must be balanced with self- awareness. The fine line between confidence and arrogance is one that many people unknowingly cross, often with negative consequences. Arrogance, or an inflated sense of one's abilities, can lead to careless decisions and a refusal to accept advice or feedback from others.

To ensure your confidence remains grounded, it is important to practice humility. A confident individual knows their strengths but also acknowledges their limitations. This blend of confidence and humility creates a balanced approach, allowing you to remain open to learning and growth. Moreover, confidence in your business and the quality of your products or services translates into stronger relationships with clients, partners, and stakeholders. It instils trust and makes others more likely to believe in your vision. Ultimately, the power of self-confidence lies not only in what you can achieve but also in how you inspire and uplift those around you.

Honest Hard Work

In today's fast-paced and competitive world, hard work remains an irreplaceable component of success. But it is not just about working harder; it is about working with sincerity and purpose. Honest hard work means giving your best effort, not cutting corners, and maintaining integrity in everything you do. This type of dedication is what separates true professionals from those who simply chase short-term gains. Many motivational speakers and successful professionals often emphasize the importance of hard work, and for good reason: it builds character, enhances skills, and opens doors to opportunities that shortcuts cannot. However, working hard does not mean neglecting your well-being. It is crucial to strike a balance, ensuring that your efforts are sustainable over the long term.

Burnout is a real risk when hard work turns into overwork. Therefore, a realistic and practical approach to hard work is essential. Recognize your limits and work diligently within them, understanding that progress may be slow but steady. Sometimes, even with your best efforts, outcomes may not align with your expectations. In such cases, it is important to keep a practical and balanced outlook, free from guilt or self-criticism. Instead, learn from the experience and continue putting in honest, consistent effort. This mindset builds resilience and keeps you motivated, even when faced with setbacks.

Willingness to Take Risks

Business and risk go hand in hand. To achieve success, you must be willing to take calculated risks. This does not mean diving into the unknown without preparation or making hasty decisions based on impulse. Instead, it involves a strategic approach to risk-taking, one that is grounded in thorough research, analysis, and planning. Before committing to a risky venture, gather as much information as possible. Understand the potential benefits as well as the possible downsides. Assessing risks from all angles helps you make informed choices that are more likely to yield favourable results.

Risk-taking requires a certain level of mental preparedness. It is about being ready for both success and failure, understanding that not every gamble will pay off. This readiness makes you resilient, capable of bouncing back from losses and learning from them. It is also important to have contingency plans in place. Being prepared for the worst-case scenario does not make you pessimistic; it makes you pragmatic. Taking risks with this level of awareness ensures that you are not acting recklessly but are instead making strategic moves that align with your long-term vision. Each risk you take should bring you closer to your goals, even if the journey involves a few setbacks along the way.

Curiosity and Willingness to Learn

Success in business is not a destination but a continuous journey filled with exploration, adaptation, and growth. One of the most vital skills that an entrepreneur can cultivate is a deep-rooted curiosity and an insatiable desire to learn. The world of business is constantly evolving, driven by rapid technological advancements, shifting economic trends, and the emergence of new markets. Staying relevant in such a dynamic environment requires an eagerness to keep up with the latest developments, whether they pertain to innovative technologies, market demands, or fresh strategies in economic planning. This adaptability is what separates thriving businesses from those that stagnate.

Curiosity fuels your drive to ask questions, seek out new knowledge, and approach each day with the excitement of learning something valuable. Every person you meet, every customer interaction, and even the broader societal trends offer lessons that can enrich your understanding of how your business fits into the world. Being open to learning from these experiences and applying that knowledge can set you apart and propel you forward. It's about viewing challenges not as obstacles but as opportunities for growth and development. This mindset keeps your business agile and better equipped to handle future challenges.

Financial Management

A well-thought-out financial strategy is the backbone of any successful business. Managing finances with a disciplined approach ensures that your venture remains stable, even during economic fluctuations. Effective financial planning encompasses a variety of practices, such as budgeting, monitoring expenses, and investing wisely to grow your resources. It also involves risk assessment, where you identify potential financial setbacks before they occur and take measures to mitigate them. The discipline to handle finances carefully, without succumbing to the temptation of reckless spending or poor investment choices, is key to long- term sustainability.

Imagine a business that generates significant income but has poor expense management. Over time, the lack of balance between revenue and expenditure could lead to financial instability, and ultimately, the business might collapse. Being prudent with your finances means not just managing the present but also planning for the future. Setting aside reserves for unexpected circumstances, regularly reviewing financial performance, and seeking professional advice when necessary are practices that can safeguard the health of your business. Remember, financial management is not a one-time task but an ongoing process that requires vigilance, adaptability, and forward-thinking strategies.

Building Connections with Society

In the business world, success is intricately tied to how well you connect with society. The public isn't just an audience; they are your customers, partners, and, at times, even your advocates. Building genuine, positive relationships with the people around you can significantly influence your business's success. This involves more than just offering a product or service; it's about understanding the needs and desires of your target audience and responding to them in meaningful ways. A business that values customer satisfaction and community engagement is more likely to earn trust, loyalty, and long-term support.

For example, imagine a local business that takes the time to engage with its community through events or outreach programs. Such efforts make the company feel more approachable and connected to the public, which often leads to a strong and loyal customer base. It's not merely about sales; it's about contributing to the community and forming partnerships that are mutually beneficial. Listening to customer feedback, adapting your services based on demand, and showing a commitment to the welfare of society all help in building a solid reputation. Ultimately, these connections form a crucial foundation that allows your business to thrive.

Clarity in Communication

Communication is a tool that can either make or break your business relationships. Clear and effective communication goes beyond just speaking or writing plainly; it's about conveying your ideas with precision and sincerity. In a business setting, this means being transparent about what you offer, detailing the benefits of your products or services without resorting to exaggeration or false promises. When discussing your business, choose your words thoughtfully to ensure that your message resonates well with your audience and leaves no room for misunderstandings. Clarity builds trust and minimizes confusion, making it easier for others to engage with your brand.

For instance, if you are introducing a new product, providing clear and straightforward information helps potential customers understand what makes your product unique and valuable. Even if they choose not to make a purchase immediately, your honesty leaves a positive impression, which can lead to future business. In an era where consumers are bombarded with overwhelming choices and information, being genuine and straightforward is a quality that people appreciate. Moreover, clear communication within your team ensures that everyone is aligned and working towards the same goals, reducing the likelihood of errors and enhancing productivity.

A Realistic Perspective on Success

Reflecting on years of experience, it becomes evident that there is no surefire path to guaranteed success. Each individual's journey is unique, influenced by countless variables, including luck. The idea of luck remains an elusive concept—something we cannot definitively prove but often acknowledge as a force that plays a role in life's outcomes. There are instances where a person with less preparation may succeed spectacularly, while someone who has done everything right may still face setbacks. Understanding this reality helps manage expectations and encourages resilience.

True success is less about achieving a specific milestone and more about the journey, the lessons learned, and the positive impact you make on those around you. Satisfaction comes not only from the accomplishments but also from the experience and wisdom gained along the way. Even if you don't achieve all your goals, the value of what you learn and the relationships you build cannot be underestimated. The satisfaction of contributing positively to your community or industry is just as rewarding as any financial gain or accolade.

The Essence of Perseverance and Flexibility

Rather than striving solely for success, it is more fulfilling to work towards customer satisfaction and personal growth. This means being passionate and committed but not rigid. Stubbornly chasing success at the expense of your well-being or peace of mind is neither sustainable nor healthy. Instead, focus on making an honest effort and adapting as needed. If a particular approach isn't working, be willing to reassess and pivot rather than forcing an outcome. The essence of perseverance lies in continuously striving towards your goals, but it also involves knowing when to change course for the better.

Life and business are unpredictable, full of unexpected twists and turns. Accepting this uncertainty and finding joy in the process makes the journey more enjoyable. Keep your dreams alive, aim high, and never stop pushing forward. Yet, remember to remain flexible, learn from each experience, and measure success not just by what you achieve but by the positive influence you have and the growth you experience along the way.

Know Yourself, Assess, and Move Forward

My real foundation was laid in the schools of Ruikhel and Ghogargaon (Tal. Shrigonda). In the primary school at Ruikhel, I learned to read, while at Shri Chatrapati Shivaji Vidyalaya in Ghogargaon, under the Rayat Education Society, I learned to understand what I read. During that time, I had friends like Yogesh Ugle, Sunil Jagtap, Yogesh Date, and brothers Kiran and Balu Tarte. Later, as we moved on to college, we all started looking for jobs. Meanwhile, one of our friends, Pravin Mahandule, became a doctor, while another close friend, my benchmate, Parsaram Gunjal, became a businessman at a young age. Another schoolmate, Navnath Kangle, also ventured into business.

Both Parsaram and Navnath settled in life much earlier than the rest of us. While we were still attending college, figuring out what to do and how to do it, they had already started gaining hands-on experience in business.

Parsaram's father ran a small hotel near the Ghogargaon bus stand. This meant that Parsaram already had a solid foundation in place for him. With an established space and a family background in business, he naturally gravitated towards the same field. He transformed himself completely, no longer just another student from our group but a dedicated businessman who put his energy into expanding and running the family enterprise.

Navnath Kangle, on the other hand, mastered business skills and gained recognition in the fabrication industry. When we were in school, his father used to do blacksmith work and sharecropping to support the family. By the time we reached the 11ᵗʰ grade, Navnath's elder brother, Dattatraya, had joined Joshi's Kohinoor Technical Institute. Around the year 2000, Manohar Joshi's 'Kohinoor' institute was producing highly skilled professionals who later became successful entrepreneurs. Dattatraya learned fabrication skills there and eventually started his own business. Navnath later joined him, learning the trade firsthand.

While my friends and I were struggling with competitive exams and preparing for jobs, they were already working in the real world, gaining practical experience and understanding how businesses operate. Today, Navnath is one of the most well-known fabricators in western Maharashtra, offering high-quality services.

Their stories illustrate an important point—both of them understood themselves, assessed their strengths, and found their own path. They did not waste time comparing themselves to others or worrying about how their peers were securing jobs. Instead, they committed to their chosen field, acquired skills, and steadily progressed.

Another friend, Vaibhav Dhasal, also followed this principle. After college, he started by selling sugarcane bundles, then moved on to agricultural service centers, and now runs a multi-crore business. His detailed journey is covered in another chapter, but his story, too, is about self-awareness, adaptation, and overcoming negativity. He embraced change, let go of negative thoughts, and refined his strengths, which ultimately led to his success.

To move forward in life, one must be willing to fight, learn, and take risks. It is this internal drive that shapes one's journey.

The Right Opportunity for the Right Person

There are hundreds of books written about Chatrapati Shivaji Maharaj, and many movies have depicted his life in great detail. But was he great simply because he wielded a sword and won battles? The answer is no.

While he was an exceptional warrior, his true success lay in his governance, strategy, and ability to empower the right people. Many warriors existed before and after him, but Shivaji's greatness was in his leadership—his ability to trust his people, care for his subjects, and ensure equality and justice for all. His decisions in administration and governance were what made his empire last.

One of his greatest strengths was appointing the right person for the right job. He recognized talent, nurtured it, and placed individuals in roles where they could excel.

Take Bahirji Naik, for example. He was a raw talent, but Shivaji Maharaj polished him into a brilliant strategist. Under Shivaji's guidance, Bahirji and his team became the eyes and ears of the Maratha empire. Running an intelligence network is not just about gathering information; it requires skillful leadership and an understanding of human nature. Shivaji Maharaj ensured that Bahirji's talent was utilized to its full potential.

Similarly, in his Ashtapradhan Mandal (Council of Eight Ministers), Shivaji Maharaj appointed individuals based on their strengths. Moropant Pingle, a visionary leader, was made Prime Minister (Pradhan) because he was skilled in governance and administration. His expertise in policy-making and agricultural development helped the kingdom prosper.

The dream of Swarajya, planted by Shahaji Maharaj and nurtured by Rajmata Jijabai, needed a strong team to bring it to life. Shivaji Maharaj carefully selected and empowered his ministers, generals, and administrators, ensuring that every individual in his court was placed where they could make the biggest impact. This strategic delegation was the foundation on which the Maratha empire was built.

The lesson here is clear—self-awareness is the first step to success. Once you understand your strengths and weaknesses, you can choose the right path, develop your skills, and commit to your journey with confidence. Whether in business or in life, the key is to recognize where you belong and pursue it wholeheartedly.

CHAPTER EIGHT

Choosing the Right Business Strategy is Crucial

Embarking on the journey to become a successful professional begins in the mind. It is there that we first nurture dreams, generate innovative ideas, and lay the foundation of our business plans. Bringing these visions to life involves more than just enthusiasm; it requires choosing a business that aligns both with our capabilities and the demands of the market. Yet, it's common for individuals to leap into business ventures with the unrealistic hope that someone else will hold their hand through every step, effectively "spoon-feeding" them. This approach can often lead to disappointment. Even if a person gives their all, businesses founded on such dependency tend to fail, resulting in a high rate of business failures.

On the flip side, businesses rooted in our genuine passions, built on a foundation that addresses societal and customer needs, have a significantly greater chance of succeeding. The key lies in strategic alignment—matching what you love and excel at with the actual needs of the community and market. It is worth noting that the size or scale of a business does not inherently determine its value or potential. What matters is the effort, dedication, and relevance you bring to your chosen venture. Many people, for example, get inspired by large, successful jewellery showrooms like Tanishq or global giants like P&G and dream of launching glamorous enterprises. But pouring money into a flashy setup doesn't guarantee success. Choosing the right business requires thoughtful analysis and a clear understanding of your strengths and market requirements. Everyone has the potential to become a successful entrepreneur, but it is crucial to select a business that matches your skill set, passion, and practical qualifications. Let's dive deeper with an illustrative story.

No Compromise in Learning

Fifteen years ago, I left Pune-Mumbai to relocate to Nagar with a vision to work in rural development. My dream was to empower farmers and guide self-help groups in building sustainable business models. However, I lacked formal education in this field at the time, and the overly ambitious nature of my partners led us to expand rapidly throughout Maharashtra. Sadly, the business collapsed, and we faced defeat. The reasons for this failure are linked to the nuances of working in partnerships, which I will discuss later. But during this time, a classmate of mine, someone equally talented in academics, embarked on his own journey. Like many young entrepreneurs, he had plenty of ideas but no concrete direction. It's a truth of life that finding the right path often involves facing failures and, more importantly, learning from them.

After he completed his studies, my friend faced two choices: take a conventional job or dive into entrepreneurship. He opted for the latter and opened an agricultural service centre. Even during college, he had always been fascinated by tractors and the farming process. He would use his own tractor to transport fodder for sugarcane fields, putting in hard work without any hesitation. This love for agriculture and machinery made his work feel more like a passion than a burden. Today, his enthusiasm remains unchanged. He had an innate ability to connect with farmers and their families, conversing with ease and understanding their challenges. His brother, an agriculture graduate, shared his passion, and together, they were always exploring new technologies. Their curiosity and eagerness to learn drove their business forward, whether it was through academic studies, friendly competitions, or entrepreneurial ventures.

Don't Stop After a Setback

Starting an agricultural service centre is not uncommon, and my friend embarked on this venture with great zeal. What set him apart was his willingness to learn about emerging technologies and his ability to engage meaningfully with farmers and agricultural officers. He was not content to merely sell agricultural inputs. Instead, he sought to deepen his understanding of effective communication and service delivery. He even leveraged his connections with political figures, using their influence in strategic and responsible ways. His business was built on a shared vision that took into account the aspirations of his entire team, ensuring that everyone's input was valued and respected.

Eventually, his journey led him to explore opportunities in drip irrigation, especially as the agricultural department's micro-irrigation scheme was gaining traction. Around the same time, the government introduced policies promoting protected farming techniques, such as shade netting and polyhouses. This was a transformative moment for farmers who grew flowers, vegetables, or maintained nurseries. The potential of protected farming was immense, seen as a significant boon that promised increased yields and more efficient farming methods. Seizing this opportunity, his team researched the concept thoroughly, established contacts with both multinational and Indian companies, and prepared to build a business around it.

As they made initial strides, he crossed paths with a manager from a prominent company who became a source of inspiration and mentorship. Encouraged by this newfound guidance, he decided to take a bold step: launching his own polyhouse construction company. Despite his lack of prior experience, his drive to explore this new avenue was strong. However, the harsh realities of business soon hit hard. The very manager he had trusted and relied upon turned out to be unreliable, and the venture suffered a major setback.

This setback was not merely a financial blow but a moment of deep reflection and learning. It taught him that in business, setbacks are inevitable, and the path to success is often riddled with challenges. But those who persevere, adapt, and learn from their failures are the ones who ultimately find success. His journey serves as a reminder that the road to building a successful business is rarely straightforward. It requires a blend of passion, resilience, adaptability, and continuous learning.

Don't Give Up After a Setback

The family faced immense challenges, putting everything they had on the line for their business. They took out personal and bank loans and invested heavily in inventory, only to see it accumulate while customers remained elusive. The weight of the financial burden and the uncertainty of their future brought a cloud of anxiety and disillusionment. The once hopeful question, "What should we do next?" began to feel haunting, and every sleepless night was marked by doubts and fear. Yet, in the face of immense frustration and despair, they made a conscious decision to persevere as a united front. They resolved to keep fighting, not as isolated individuals but as a cohesive team bound by determination and shared purpose.

The early days were far from easy. Like any startup journey, the initial phase was filled with scepticism and ridicule from onlookers. They faced mockery and discouragement, but they clung to each other for motivation, offering words of encouragement, playful teasing, and relentless support. They embraced the realization that when life forces you to innovate, the human spirit can be incredibly resilient. They learned that solutions often come from unexpected sources, including family, friends, and a deeper reservoir of strength within themselves. Their inner drive and unwavering teamwork pulled them through.

This group, which began in the rural areas of Maharashtra, eventually transformed their setbacks into opportunities. They not only survived but thrived, evolving into a reputable and reliable company. Today, Agrovision Greenhouse Construction Company (AVGC) stands as a testament to their perseverance. It has grown to become the largest wholesaler of shade nets and polyhouses in Maharashtra, with a turnover that runs into crores. Their journey from near-collapse to industry leadership is an inspiring story of resilience and innovation.

Dream Big, but Start Small

Every successful business begins with understanding who your target consumers are and what needs you can fulfil. When starting out, it is essential to offer services or products that are not only high in quality but also reliable and relevant. Take the time to make a detailed list of potential products or services and assess whether there is genuine demand in the market. Don't rush into the business world without carefully analysing the needs of your audience. Seek the guidance of experienced professionals from different industries, including fellow business owners and service providers. Present your business concepts to them and actively listen to their feedback. Their insights might highlight potential challenges or risks that you hadn't considered.

It's important to take these concerns seriously. Think critically about how these risks could impact your business, and brainstorm ways to minimize them. Have thoughtful discussions with people who are enthusiastic about your idea to understand what aspects they find most promising and how you can further refine your strategy. This feedback loop will help clarify your vision and prepare you for the realities of the market.

Once you are confident in your business plan, the next step is to assess the opportunities it presents. Consider the timeline for achieving your financial and social goals, the level of investment required, and whether pursuing this path is a worthwhile endeavour. Ask yourself hard questions: Will this venture meet your long-term aspirations? If you're still unsure, engage in conversations with critics or sceptics who can point out potential flaws in your plan. Their doubts can be eye-opening and guide you to make better, more informed decisions. Remember, perfection in planning is unattainable. Aim instead for a balanced and realistic strategy that sets you up for sustainable growth.

When your idea feels solid, and you've identified your target market, it's time to consider the necessary investments. Starting a business requires both financial resources and human capital. However, avoid making substantial investments simply because you have funds at your disposal or because you expect an easy return on investment. It's crucial to immerse yourself in the field, gaining practical experience before committing large sums of money. Ideally, spend three to five years in the industry—either as an employee or as a hands-on business owner—to truly understand the market dynamics and challenges.

Starting small doesn't diminish the value of your venture. In fact, many successful enterprises have had humble beginnings. For instance, consider Asha Bhel, a small snack shop that started as a highway food stall in Ahmednagar. Over time, it expanded into a chain of restaurants with multiple locations, capturing a substantial share of the market. Likewise, Sopanrao Wadewale, Joshi Wadewale, and Chitale Bandhu are examples of businesses that started modestly. These ventures steadily grew by delivering consistent quality and earning the trust of their customers. Their success stories show that starting small and scaling up strategically can lead to remarkable growth.

However, aspiring entrepreneurs often fall into the trap of overestimating their capabilities and attempting to compete directly with established industry giants. This can lead to poor decision-making, such as making large, premature investments without a full understanding of the business landscape. Running a business is not just about having money to invest; it also demands physical stamina, mental resilience, and a willingness to work through the smallest details.

Take the example of successful restaurant owners in Pune, Kolhapur, and Ahmednagar. They are not just business managers; they are experts in the culinary arts. They have worked tirelessly to learn the intricacies of their craft, from perfecting recipes to creating memorable dining experiences for their customers. Managing a restaurant involves much more than overseeing finances and operations. It requires a deep understanding of customer preferences, kitchen management, and the overall ambiance. Creating an exceptional experience requires skill, patience, and a genuine passion for the work.

The lesson here is clear: success comes from starting small, working hard, and growing gradually while learning from every experience. Dream big, but always be willing to start from the ground up and build your vision one step at a time.

The Benefits of Starting Small

When it comes to launching a new business, starting on a smaller scale can offer numerous advantages that are often overlooked in the rush to achieve grand ambitions. One of the most significant benefits is the ability to enter the market without exposing yourself to substantial financial risk. In a small-scale business, your initial investment is typically more manageable, which means that if your venture doesn't yield the expected results, the financial consequences are not devastating. This aspect of minimized risk provides a cushion, giving you the flexibility to pivot, adapt, or even exit the business, if necessary, without severe repercussions.

Beyond financial safety, starting small offers an unparalleled opportunity to learn and grow as an entrepreneur. When you're running a smaller operation, you naturally become involved in every facet of the business. You will handle a wide range of responsibilities, from dealing with suppliers to managing customer service, marketing, sales, and even troubleshooting technical issues. This hands-on experience is incredibly valuable, as it helps you develop a diverse skill set. You'll learn firsthand how to allocate resources efficiently, address customer concerns, and solve problems creatively and effectively. These lessons form a solid foundation that will serve you well as you expand your business in the future.

Another crucial benefit of beginning on a smaller scale is the ability to foster direct and meaningful relationships with your customers. Because your business is more intimate, you can engage with your clients on a personal level, which allows you to gain a deeper understanding of their needs, preferences, and pain points. This connection is vital because customer feedback can act as a powerful guide for improving your products or services. By being attentive and adaptable, you can fine-tune your offerings, build loyalty, and establish a reputation for excellent customer service. In essence, your early customers become partners in your growth, offering insights and feedback that can make your business more successful in the long run.

It is also highly beneficial to gain experience by working for someone else in the same industry before venturing out on your own. Whether you take a role as an employee or gain practical exposure through an internship or part-time work, the insights you'll gain are often priceless. You'll learn the nuances of the business, understand industry standards, and observe how seasoned professionals handle various challenges. This experience will not only boost your confidence but also prepare you to navigate the complexities of running your own business. You'll be better equipped to anticipate problems, make informed decisions, and lead your enterprise to success.

Understanding the Realities of Business

While the benefits of entrepreneurship are numerous, it's essential to approach business with a clear understanding of the challenges involved. Starting and running a business is not for the faint of heart. Every day, you'll encounter new hurdles and unexpected problems that require swift and thoughtful solutions. The reality of entrepreneurship is that it demands persistence, resilience, and a willingness to keep moving forward even when the path is difficult. If you're not prepared to face these challenges head-on, it may be wise to reconsider your entrepreneurial aspirations. Success in business never comes easily, but with a determined mindset and a readiness to adapt, you can overcome obstacles and build a business that stands the test of time.

This guide does not aim to cover the complexities of corporate culture or the intricacies of managing large-scale enterprises. Instead, it focuses on the fundamentals of building a business from the ground up. It offers practical, actionable advice for those who are either launching their first venture or looking to grow a small business into a more substantial operation. The corporate world and large-scale business strategies are best reserved for those who have already established themselves and have the resources to navigate that space effectively. This book is dedicated to the everyday entrepreneur—the dreamer who wants to make their vision a reality, step by manageable step.

Whether your ambition is to run a thriving local business or to expand it into a larger enterprise over time, the key is to start where you are, use what you have, and learn along the way. By understanding the benefits of starting small and preparing for the realities of the business world, you can set a strong foundation for future success. Remember, even the largest companies once began as humble startups. With dedication, adaptability, and a commitment to continuous learning, you can transform your small idea into something extraordinary.

Key Considerations for Choosing a Business:

Passion and Choice

When choosing a business, it's vital to reflect on your personal interests and passions. What excites you? What activities do you find enjoyable, and how can you turn those interests into professional success? Passion is a driving force that fuels the energy and dedication required to succeed. Starting a business demands a high level of adaptability; you'll need to adjust your mindset and approach according to the nature of the business you choose. However, there's a balance to be struck. While working on something you're passionate about can bring immense satisfaction, it's important not to fall into the trap of pursuing a business that does not align with your interests or strengths. This could lead to burnout and add you to the list of failed entrepreneurs who were unable to sustain their initial enthusiasm.

Doing something you love makes the challenges of business more bearable and can keep you motivated during tough times. However, pursuing a venture that doesn't resonate with your values or doesn't ignite your passion can lead to frustration and a lack of fulfillment. Remember, businesses that thrive tend to be built by those who are genuinely passionate about what they do—people who see beyond the struggles and focus on the long-term vision.

Market Study

Market research is a fundamental pillar for business success. It should never be an afterthought. In fact, it's crucial to conduct thorough market research before you even start your business, and this analysis should continue throughout the life of your business. The business landscape is always changing, and customer preferences, product demand, and market conditions are in constant flux. A solid understanding of the market before you launch will give you the insights needed to make informed decisions, but that's not the end of the process. Ongoing market study allows you to stay ahead of competitors and adapt to new trends, helping you stay relevant as customer needs evolve.

A key part of market research is understanding your target audience—their needs, behaviours, and pain points. Analysing competitors and tracking industry trends will allow you to pinpoint gaps in the market and develop products or services that are uniquely positioned to address these needs. Regularly revisiting this analysis as your business grows will help you stay responsive and agile, ensuring that your business doesn't become stagnant.

Understanding Future Trends

Having a clear vision for the future is essential, regardless of the size of the business you are starting. Whether it's a small kiosk, a food stall, or a larger enterprise, running a business is about more than just day-to-day operations; it's about preparing for what comes next. Understanding market trends and technological advancements is critical to maintaining long- term success. If you are not anticipating future changes, your business might fall behind, just as many once-prominent brands like Nokia, Onida TVs, or Daewoo Motors did. These companies were leaders in their industries, but they failed to adapt to changing technologies and evolving consumer needs, leading to their downfall.

To run a sustainable business, you need to forecast what's ahead. You must keep an eye on developments in your industry, anticipate shifts in consumer behaviour, and be ready to embrace new technologies that can help you streamline operations or improve your products. Whether it's the rise of e-commerce, the adoption of artificial intelligence, or shifts toward sustainability, staying informed and adaptable is essential to long-term success.

Big Dreams, Small Start—Or Not

Many successful entrepreneurs begin with the mindset of starting small and growing steadily over time. This approach allows for a manageable risk and the opportunity to learn the ropes gradually. However, starting small does not always apply to every business model. If you have a deep understanding of the business you want to enter, a well-trained and capable workforce, and the financial readiness to invest in scaling up quickly, there's no harm in starting on a larger scale. In some industries, rapid growth might be necessary to stay competitive, and launching big from the beginning can be a viable strategy if you're well- prepared.

Even if you plan to scale rapidly, it's essential to have a clear exit strategy in place. This will ensure that if things don't go as planned, you are prepared with a well-defined course of action. An exit plan is a vital safety net that provides peace of mind and helps mitigate risk.

Consulting Experts: Finding the Right Guidance

When seeking advice for your business, it's important to engage with professionals who offer diverse perspectives. Many marketing consultants might advise you to take high risks, such as taking loans to scale quickly, with the goal of rapidly capturing market share. While these strategies can work for some, they don't suit every business model and can lead to significant financial strain if not managed correctly.

It's equally important to consult with business experts who can provide broader, more practical advice that focuses not just on marketing but on the operational, financial, and strategic aspects of running a business. Engage with both marketing and business consultants, asking questions from every angle and challenging their advice. This well-rounded approach will provide you with a clearer understanding of the risks, benefits, and realistic expectations of your business plan. With thorough guidance, you'll be in a better position to make an informed decision.

Persistence, Hard Work, and Continuous Learning

Success in business doesn't come overnight. It requires dedication, perseverance, and the willingness to keep learning. Continuous self-education is essential to stay relevant in a fast-changing business world. Commit to improving your knowledge of your industry, staying up-to-date with new technologies and trends, and learning from both successes and failures. Building a business is a long-term journey, and only by staying focused, adapting to new challenges, and growing as an entrepreneur will you see lasting success.

Ultimately, success comes from following a structured process, making informed decisions, and staying true to your vision. Keep pushing forward, refining your strategies, and learning from every step you take—this persistence and willingness to learn are what truly separate successful entrepreneurs from those who fall short.

Turning Business into a Dream Through Consistency

Ahmednagar's food culture is renowned across Maharashtra. People from Pune, Mumbai, and Marathwada drive over 200 kilometers just to indulge in its signature spicy black mutton curry. Some of the most famous eateries include Hotel Sandeep in Kedgaon, Hotel Sagam and Pragati in Maliwada, and the legendary Rambharose Khanawal—all favourites among meat lovers. Other iconic spots like Phule Hotel near Rahuri Agricultural University and Rashin's Pala-style mutton kanduri also have a loyal fan base.

One such name that has grown into a business empire through sheer consistency and adaptation is Asha Bhel.

This beloved eatery started humbly in 1963 at Pandhari Pool, located on Aurangabad (now Chatrapati Sambhajinagar) Road. The late Shantilalji Banberu first set up a small roadside stall selling bhel, completely unaware that it would become a franchise-driven business empire in the future.

Back then, Pandhari Pool was just another stop on the road. But as traffic increased between Ahmednagar and Aurangabad, and industrial activity expanded in Ghodegaon, the marketplace around Pandhari Pool flourished. Asha Bhel's unique, flavourful snack quickly gained a loyal following, and as demand grew, so did the business. Over time, many other vendors set up shop nearby, but Asha Bhel retained its reputation through quality and consistency.

With the next generation at the helm, the business has adapted to modern trends, recognizing the power of social media and franchise marketing. They expanded using a chain model, establishing new outlets across Maharashtra. Today, Asha Bhel is no longer just a local stall—it's a statewide brand with a growing presence.

Their story is proof that any business, no matter how small, can achieve great success through perseverance and adaptability.

Success does not follow a fixed formula, just as failure is never guaranteed. However, losing focus and getting distracted by non-productive activities almost always leads to downfall. On the other hand, maintaining consistency, quality, and a clear vision significantly increases the chances of success.

Every business requires constant learning and strategic evolution to thrive. Asha Bhel has done exactly that, and their commitment to growth is evident. They have now launched a website, expanded their franchise network, and are helping new entrepreneurs enter the food industry under their brand.

Their journey serves as an inspiration—sustained effort, adaptability, and a commitment to quality can turn even the simplest business into a thriving success story.

CHAPTER NINE

Advantages and Disadvantages of Sole Proprietorship or OPC (One Person Company)

When starting a business, many individuals begin their entrepreneurial journey alone. However, even in these early stages, friendships or acquaintances may lead to future partnerships. Often, businesses evolve from being a sole proprietorship into a partnership as the need for additional resources or skills arises. In this section, we'll explore the concept of a Sole Proprietorship, where one individual owns and operates the business. This can also include a One Person Company (OPC), which is a registered form of sole proprietorship but with more formal structure and benefits.

Advantages of Sole Proprietorship

1. Complete Control

One of the biggest advantages of a sole proprietorship is the complete control over the business. As the sole owner, you have the freedom to make decisions quickly, adapt to changes swiftly, and implement your ideas without the need to consult anyone else. This autonomy allows you to shape your business in the way you envision it, making decisions based on your own goals and priorities. However, this control also means you are solely responsible for the outcomes—both successes and failures. While this can be daunting, it also provides an opportunity to develop a strong sense of responsibility and leadership.

As the only person in charge, you'll need to address all challenges on your own. If there are issues within the business, there's no one else to blame—everything falls on you. This fosters a deep sense of accountability, helping you refine your decision-making skills. Moreover, over time, you'll develop strategies to overcome weaknesses and errors in the business, honing your skills to ensure that you don't make the same mistakes twice.

2. Profits and Investments Are All Yours

Another significant advantage of a sole proprietorship is that profits and investments are entirely yours. Since you are the sole owner of the business, you have complete control over how the profits are utilized. You can reinvest the earnings into the business or take them as personal income, based on your priorities. The financial freedom that comes with this setup can be very appealing, especially for those looking to create a self-sustaining business.

At the same time, this means that losses are also your responsibility. The onus is on you to manage the finances wisely, ensuring that unnecessary expenses are avoided. A sole proprietorship teaches financial discipline because the owner is directly impacted by the financial success or failure of the business. Gradually, this leads to more careful decision- making and prudent management of resources.

This model allows you to start small with a minimal investment and grow at your own pace. Without the need to consult partners or investors, you have the flexibility to make decisions that align with your vision, whether you're expanding gradually or scaling up when you feel confident.

3. Simple Management

A major benefit of operating a sole proprietorship is the simplicity of management. With only one person responsible for running the business, there is no need to engage in time- consuming discussions or debates with partners or stakeholders. Decisions can be made quickly, allowing for greater agility in adapting to market changes or customer needs.

Additionally, because the management structure is so streamlined, you don't have to worry about the complexities of organizing meetings, delegating tasks, or navigating disagreements between multiple parties. This level of simplicity extends to the business's financial and operational matters. Since you are the only one handling these aspects, confidential information and business strategies remain secure and under your control, reducing the risk of leaks or misunderstandings.

Without partners or a board of directors, the business structure remains uncomplicated, which makes it easier to stay focused on the day-to-day tasks and long-term goals without unnecessary distractions. This straightforward approach to running a business is often a key factor in the success of many small-scale ventures, particularly those in their early stages.

Disadvantages of Sole Proprietorship:

While the sole proprietorship model offers several advantages, it also comes with its own set of challenges. The disadvantages of running a sole proprietorship can affect both the day-to-day operations and long-term sustainability of the business. Here are some key drawbacks:

1.

Risk and Responsibility Fall Entirely on You

One of the most significant disadvantages of a sole proprietorship is the complete responsibility you bear for the business. As the only decision-maker, you have to take on all the risks, whether they are financial, operational, or legal. If your business is successful, you enjoy all the rewards; however, if it fails or incurs losses, you bear the full brunt of the financial and emotional strain. This can be a heavy burden to carry, particularly when things aren't going well.

Because you are the sole owner, all aspects of the business—from making decisions, managing finances, overseeing employee performance, to maintaining product quality—rest solely on your shoulders. As the business grows, handling these multiple areas by yourself can become overwhelming. You may not have the expertise in every aspect of business management, which could impact your ability to manage everything effectively. Moreover, the stress of managing every decision on your own can sometimes lead to burnout or poor decision-making.

2.

Capital Constraints

Another disadvantage of a sole proprietorship is limited access to capital. When starting a business, you likely have limited financial resources. In a partnership, the pooled resources of multiple people help mitigate financial constraints, but in a sole proprietorship, you are limited to your own funds or the money you can personally secure through loans or savings. This restriction can hinder your ability to scale the business, invest in new technologies, expand product offerings, or hire more employees.

As the business grows, the need for additional capital becomes more pressing. Without the ability to easily raise funds through investors or partners, you may find it difficult to make significant expansions or diversifications. This can result in missed opportunities for growth or improvements, which can restrict the potential of your business in the long run. The reliance on limited personal finances may also make you more hesitant to take necessary risks, further slowing down progress.

3.

Difficulty in Identifying and Seizing Larger Opportunities

A sole proprietorship can also face difficulties when it comes to identifying and capitalizing on larger opportunities. While you may be adept at running the day-to-day operations, growing a business requires a strong team and specialized skills. As the only person running the show, you may find it difficult to focus on both the operational and strategic aspects of the business simultaneously. This can hinder your ability to spot larger, more lucrative opportunities in the market.

Even if you do identify these opportunities, the lack of skilled employees or managers to help you execute the necessary strategies can be a significant limitation. For example, while you may have the vision for expansion, it may be challenging to manage the logistics of such growth by yourself. Skilled professionals or managers are essential to guide the business through phases of growth. Without them, you risk stalling at a certain point, limiting the business's potential. Furthermore, even experienced managers might leave to start their own ventures, creating gaps in leadership and continuity. This unpredictability can prevent the business from scaling as easily as it might with a partner or team of committed collaborators.

Key Considerations for Starting a Sole Proprietorship:

When starting a sole proprietorship or a single-owner private limited company (OPC), there are several critical aspects to consider that will help you manage risks and set up a successful business. Here are four key points to guide you:

1.

Business Plan

A solid business plan is the foundation of any successful business, especially for a sole proprietorship. It's important to not only choose the right type of registration (sole proprietorship or OPC) but also to lay out a detailed roadmap for how your business will operate. This plan should cover several key elements:

- Management: How will the business be run on a day-to-day basis? This includes decision-making processes, delegation of tasks (if applicable), and setting goals for growth.
- Financial Handling: Clearly define how you will manage your costs, handle revenue, and track profits. Set up systems to ensure that the business remains financially stable.
- Growth Strategy: Outline the steps for scaling the business. This could include new product launches, entering new markets, or hiring additional help. A scalable business model ensures long-term success.
- Anticipating Challenges: Predict potential obstacles, such as cash flow issues, market changes, or operational setbacks, and devise strategies to overcome them. Having a plan in place for challenges can prevent you from being caught off guard.

2.

Start Small

Starting small is one of the smartest strategies when launching a business. It reduces the financial risks and allows you to learn from early mistakes without jeopardizing your entire venture. Starting on a smaller scale gives you the flexibility to adjust your business model, strategy, and operations as you progress. You can learn what works, what doesn't, and what needs to be improved. As you gain confidence and insights into the market, you can then gradually scale your business. Small beginnings allow you to test the waters, build a customer base, and establish your brand without overcommitting to large investments early on.

3.

Increase Knowledge and Skills

Running a successful business requires a wide range of skills, including sales, management, financial planning, and strategy. It's crucial to continually invest time and effort into developing these skills. Operating a sole proprietorship means you'll often be responsible for all aspects of the business, so knowledge in different areas is key.

- Dedicate time to self-study, whether it's reading books, attending workshops, or engaging in online courses related to business management, marketing, finance, and customer service.
- Engage in continuous learning, reflecting on your own experiences and seeking feedback from others to improve your decision-making and problem-solving abilities.
- Strategic thinking will also be essential as you navigate challenges and opportunities, and it's something that can be honed over time with practice and focus.

4.

Make Wise Investments

Managing capital wisely is one of the most important aspects of running a successful sole proprietorship. It can be tempting to make flashy investments to impress others or to establish your business as an immediate success, but it's important to focus on long-term sustainability. Consider the following:

- Strategic investments: Use your available capital to invest in areas that will directly contribute to the growth and stability of the business. This could mean investing in quality materials, marketing strategies, or technology that streamlines operations.
- Risk assessment: Every investment carries risks, so it's crucial to assess the potential rewards against the possible downsides. Consider your personal financial obligations and the impact of each investment on both your business and your life.
- Balancing reinvestment and risk management: While it's important to reinvest profits into your business for growth, it's equally important to maintain a healthy balance by setting aside funds for unexpected expenses or financial downturns. Being cautious about where and how much you invest will allow you to weather any future business challenges.

By focusing on these key considerations, you will not only minimize risk but also set a solid foundation for your business to grow and thrive over time. A carefully planned, well- executed approach will increase your chances of long-term success in the competitive world of business.

Not Just 'Ekla Chalo,' But 'Sabke Saath Chalo'

One person alone may not be able to change the world, but a single individual can certainly set the wheels of change in motion. We've all heard this sentiment before. The same principle applies to business. The vision of an individual often sparks the birth of a great enterprise, but to bring that vision to life, it is essential to build the right team.

A recent example of this is the IPO launch of PNG Jewellers—a Pune-based jewelry giant. Investors showed tremendous faith in the company, leading to a successful stock market debut. This means PNG will now expand further, creating more employment opportunities while also bringing profits to shareholders. What makes this company stand out is that even as it grows into a corporate entity, the Gadgil family remains at its core, ensuring stability and continuity.

The Journey of PNG Jewellers: From Humble Beginnings to a National Brand

Founded in 1832 by Ganesh Gadgil in Sangli, PNG started as a small roadside jewelry shop. For the first three decades, they did not even have a permanent store. After his passing, his son Narayan Gadgil continued the business, followed by the next generations.

However, it wasn't until 1958, when Anant Gadgil (popularly known as Dajikaka) opened their first showroom on Laxmi Road, Pune, that PNG truly became a recognizable brand. The business continued to evolve, and after Dajikaka's passing, his grandson Saurabh Gadgil took the company to new heights. Under his leadership, PNG transformed from a family-run business into a corporate empire with a presence in Mumbai, Goa, and even the United States. Today, with 40+ stores across multiple cities, PNG successfully launched an IPO in 2024, further cementing its position in the market.

Their 180-year legacy is proof that success does not happen overnight. Many entrepreneurs expect global recognition within a year or two of launching a business, but the PNG story shows that true growth requires decades of persistence, strategic expansion, and strong leadership.

Even back in the 1860s, PNG gained prestige when the Patwardhan royal family of Sangli named them their official jewelers. This royal patronage gave them a significant boost. Similar opportunities come to businesses today as well—but only those who seize them, innovate, and maintain quality carve their names in history.

However, it wasn't just an individual effort. Their success was built on teamwork—from managers and craftsmen to sales representatives, each played a role in making PNG the iconic brand it is today. This is why the principle "Not just Ekla Chalo, but Sabke Saath Chalo" is essential in business.

Many great enterprises, from Reliance and Adani to Jindal, have succeeded not just through individual brilliance but by fostering strong teams and leadership networks.

The Global Inspiration: The Story of Louis Vuitton

Another legendary business that follows this principle is Louis Vuitton, a brand that has redefined luxury worldwide. Regardless of economic trends, one name always appears in the list of the world's richest people—Bernard Arnault, the man behind Louis Vuitton.

Today, Louis Vuitton is synonymous with exclusivity, sophistication, and wealth, selling high-end handbags, wallets, and fashion accessories worth millions. However, few know the humble beginnings of this global empire.

Louis Vuitton was born in 1821 in a small French village called Anchay. His childhood was far from privileged. Tired of his stepmother's cruelty, he ran away from home at the age of 13, walking nearly 400 kilometers to Paris. The journey took two years, during which he survived by taking odd jobs and observing the world around him.

Once in Paris, he became an apprentice to Maréchal, a renowned trunk-maker and packing specialist. During this time, he realized that travel trunks were bulky and inconvenient, so he designed lightweight, durable, and waterproof trunks. In 1854, he founded 'Louis Vuitton Malletier', introducing an entirely new style of luggage to the world.

Even then, the brand's true rise came when he was appointed as the official trunk-maker for the French royal court, serving Empress Eugénie de Montijo, the wife of Napoleon III. This royal endorsement elevated the brand's reputation, making it the preferred choice for aristocrats across Europe.

What set Louis Vuitton apart was his commitment to quality and innovation. He never compromised on craftsmanship, refused shortcuts, and built his business on excellence rather than mass production.

However, like many family-run businesses, the next generation struggled to maintain its legacy. By the late 20th century, the brand was at risk of fading. But in 1987, it merged with Moët Hennessy, creating LVMH (Louis Vuitton Moët Hennessy)—a luxury powerhouse spanning multiple industries, including fashion, jewelry, watches, and perfumes.

Today, LVMH is the world's leading luxury brand conglomerate. What began as a poor boy's dream turned into a global empire, all because of his determination, craftsmanship, and refusal to settle for mediocrity.

The Power of a Strong Team and Long-Term Vision

Both PNG Jewellers and Louis Vuitton are proof that great businesses are not built by individuals alone. Vision and leadership matter, but sustained growth requires a strong team, adaptability, and a commitment to quality.

Many entrepreneurs dream of overnight success, but building a lasting brand takes time. Those who succeed are the ones who:

- Stay committed to their craft
- Embrace innovation while maintaining quality
- Surround themselves with the right people
- Think long-term rather than chasing quick profits

Therefore, a successful business is never about 'Ekla Chalo' (walking alone), but about 'Sabke Saath Chalo' (walking together).

CHAPTER TEN

Advantages and Disadvantages of Partnership Business

In the previous section, we explored the concept of sole proprietorship, where a single individual owns and operates a business. Now, we will delve into another popular business structure—the partnership. A partnership is a business arrangement in which two or more individuals come together to run a business. This model relies heavily on collaboration, as partners share the responsibilities of managing and growing the business. Unlike a sole proprietorship, where decision-making rests solely on one individual, a partnership distributes these duties, allowing for greater cooperation.

Partnerships are commonly seen in many industries, including construction, where businesses may appear as sole proprietorships legally but are often managed and operated as partnerships in practice. These partnerships may be formalized as Limited Liability Partnerships (LLPs), Private Limited Companies, or Limited Companies, depending on the specific legal and financial structure chosen by the partners. Even in cases where a business is legally classified as a sole proprietorship, in practice, it may still function as a partnership, especially when family members or close associates are involved in the management and decision-making processes.

In a partnership, each partner contributes resources, expertise, and capital and shares in the ownership, profits, and losses of the business. Partners are expected to contribute either equally or as agreed upon in the partnership agreement, which helps ensure fairness and clarity in the business relationship.

Advantages of Partnership Business:

Higher Capital Investment

One of the most significant advantages of a partnership is the ability to pool resources, which allows for a larger capital investment compared to a sole proprietorship. The combined financial contributions of multiple partners enable the business to start on a larger scale, with greater capacity to expand and operate in more diverse markets. This increased capital base is essential for businesses that require substantial upfront investments for equipment, technology, or facilities. The collaborative nature of the partnership ensures that the business is well-equipped to handle the challenges of the marketplace.

Shared Responsibilities and Risk Management

In a partnership, responsibilities and duties are divided among the partners, which helps alleviate the pressure on any single individual. This shared workload not only reduces physical and mental strain but also ensures that the partners are better equipped to manage the complexities of the business. Since each partner contributes their skills and expertise to different aspects of the business, the overall workload is balanced, leading to greater efficiency. The distribution of risk is another significant advantage of partnerships. If the business encounters financial difficulties or operational setbacks, the burden is shared, reducing the impact on any one partner. This creates a more sustainable business model, as the risks are spread out and mitigated through collective efforts.

Skill Management

Each partner brings their unique set of skills, knowledge, and experience to the business. This diversity in expertise is one of the key benefits of a partnership, as it enables the business to operate more effectively across multiple areas. For instance, one partner may have a strong background in accounting and finance, while another may excel in marketing or sales. When partners complement each other's strengths and address each other's weaknesses, the business can perform more efficiently, make better decisions, and minimize errors. The combination of different skill sets not only improves the operational efficiency but also enhances the business's ability to adapt to changing market conditions and challenges.

Creativity and Innovation

Partnerships foster an environment of collaboration, where diverse ideas can be shared and discussed openly. The collective knowledge and experience of the partners provide a fertile ground for innovation. When partners with different backgrounds and perspectives work together, they are more likely to come up with creative solutions to business challenges. This spirit of collaboration encourages brainstorming and problem-solving, which can lead to new product ideas, improved business strategies, or more effective ways of engaging customers. Partnerships allow for more flexible and dynamic decision-making, leading to a higher potential for innovation. By combining their resources and creativity, partners can give their business a competitive edge in the market, helping them stay ahead of the curve in terms of industry trends and customer needs.

Disadvantages of Partnership Business

While a partnership offers numerous benefits, it also comes with its own set of challenges that can hinder the smooth functioning of the business. The dynamics between partners, if not managed well, can lead to serious issues. Let's explore some of the potential drawbacks of running a partnership business:

Overexploitation of Strengths

When partners with distinct strengths come together, there is a risk that some may over- exploit their advantages at inappropriate times. While each individual brings unique capabilities to the table, they also carry their own weaknesses. A successful partnership hinges on each partner's willingness to both nurture their strengths and address their weaknesses. The partnership will only thrive if there is mutual respect, and the focus remains on the collective goal of professional success. If any partner begins to overstate their importance or leverages their strengths at the wrong time, it could destabilize the entire partnership. If these imbalances persist unchecked, they can ultimately lead to the breakdown of the business, despite any initial promise.

Conflicts and Disagreements

In any partnership, partners come with their own unique backgrounds, perspectives, and ways of thinking. It is essential to acknowledge and respect these differences for the partnership to flourish. However, when conflicts arise, they can threaten the unity of the partnership. Minor disagreements are expected, but major disputes—especially those stemming from personal egos or misunderstandings—can have disastrous consequences. These conflicts can escalate quickly and, if left unresolved, may lead to the dissolution of the partnership and the destruction of the business. Therefore, it is crucial for partners to establish a healthy communication framework and a conflict resolution strategy to avoid such scenarios.

Profit Distribution

A common point of contention in partnerships is the distribution of profits. While profit- sharing is usually based on the capital investment made by each partner, it is not always a straightforward matter. Over time, as the business grows and the contributions of each partner evolve, disagreements may surface regarding how profits should be divided. If one partner feels their contribution—be it in terms of time, effort, or expertise—is not being adequately acknowledged, tensions can rise. Such issues often result in friction and strain in the partnership, and in the worst-case scenario, they may lead to a permanent rift. To avoid these conflicts, it is essential for partners to have a clear agreement on profit-sharing from the outset, taking into account factors like time, expertise, and capital investment.

The "No Risk, Only Profit" Attitude

A significant problem arises when one or more partners adopt a mindset of "no risk, only profit." In other words, they expect to reap the rewards of the business without shouldering their fair share of the risks. This mentality can create a significant imbalance in the partnership, leading to frustration and resentment among other partners. If one partner refuses to take on their proportion of the risk but still expects to receive an equal share of the profits, it jeopardizes the long-term viability of the business. Partnerships are built on trust, and when one partner shirks their responsibilities, it can hinder growth, stifle innovation, and prevent the business from navigating challenges effectively.

Unwanted Responsibilities

In a partnership, certain decisions may carry significant risks, yet they may also yield substantial rewards. It is essential for all partners to fully understand the responsibilities they are assuming, both socially and economically, before agreeing to take on a particular role. Failure to take accountability when things go wrong can severely damage the business. Partners who adopt a "no risk, only profit" mentality often fail to fulfil their obligations, leaving others to shoulder the consequences. This irresponsibility can create a toxic atmosphere in the partnership, where one or more partners feel burdened by the work of others. Such attitudes can lead to a breakdown in cooperation and eventually destroy the business.

Difficulties in Decision-Making

A significant challenge in partnerships is the often slow and cumbersome decision- making process. Since decisions require input from all partners, reaching a consensus can be time-consuming, especially if there are disagreements or if one partner is more dominant than others. In situations where a partner's personal issues or external distractions interfere with the business, the decision-making process can be delayed even further. Prolonged indecision can cause setbacks, preventing the business from seizing opportunities or addressing problems promptly. In extreme cases, when one partner is particularly self-absorbed or believes their ideas are superior, their insistence on having the final say may lead to poor decisions that harm the business.

Difficulty in Exiting the Partnership

Exiting a partnership can be one of the most complicated and contentious processes. Unlike a sole proprietorship, where the owner has complete control over decisions, a partnership requires the cooperation of all partners to make significant changes, such as selling the business or allowing a partner to exit. If consensus is lacking or if one partner is unwilling to leave, this can trap the remaining partners in a partnership that no longer serves their interests. Disagreements over the terms of exit, the valuation of the business, or the division of assets can lead to prolonged disputes and even legal battles. Therefore, it is crucial for partners to establish an exit strategy from the outset, addressing key issues like the buyout process, valuation methods, and other contingencies to avoid future complications.

Partnership as a Business Model

Embarking on a business venture through the partnership model can be an exceptional choice, offering numerous benefits such as pooled resources, shared responsibilities, and diverse expertise. However, this approach also presents its own unique challenges. To ensure the success and longevity of a partnership, especially when working with family members or close friends, there are several key factors that need to be emphasized and adhered to. Here, we'll explore the essential elements that can help a partnership thrive:

Shared Vision and Equality

For any partnership to succeed, it is essential that all partners share a unified vision and set of values. If partners have radically different ideologies—whether political, social, or economic—it can create a fractured partnership. For instance, disagreements on key business practices, such as financial priorities or ethical concerns, can impede progress and cause irreparable damage. Thus, before forming a partnership, it is critical to ensure that there is alignment in the overall objectives, mindset, and values. This doesn't mean that all partners need to think alike in every way, but a general consensus on the direction and goals of the business is vital. When there is a common vision, partners can work together more harmoniously, propelling the business toward mutual success.

Mutual Respect and Trust

A successful partnership thrives on respect and trust. These two values form the foundation of healthy working relationships and are essential for the internal functioning of the business. The dynamics within the partnership are reflected externally in relationships with clients, vendors, and other stakeholders. Partners should appreciate each other's strengths and offer support where weaknesses exist, rather than focusing on deficiencies. Trust and respect not only create a positive work environment but also foster a sense of loyalty and accountability. When partners trust one another to carry out their responsibilities effectively, they can focus on collective goals and ensure smoother operations.

Open Communication Regarding Time and Capital Investment

An essential aspect of a successful partnership is clear and honest communication regarding the levels of time, effort, and capital that each partner brings to the business. Not all partners are able to contribute equally in every area—some may be able to invest significant capital, while others may contribute through time, skills, or expertise. Understanding and respecting these differences are crucial for setting fair expectations. Clear communication about each partner's role and investment from the beginning ensures that there are no misunderstandings about how profits and responsibilities will be divided. Open discussions about each partner's capacity to contribute can prevent future conflicts and promote a sense of fairness.

Clear Distribution of Responsibilities and Accountability

The success of a partnership hinges on the clear allocation of responsibilities. Having well-defined roles ensures that each partner knows their exact duties and obligations, which helps streamline business operations. A partnership should ideally have a formal document— often a partnership agreement—that outlines the responsibilities of each partner. This written document should detail how capital will be invested, the time commitment required from each partner, and the specific roles that each will take on. By setting expectations upfront, partners can avoid ambiguity and miscommunication. Accountability is a key aspect, as each partner must be dedicated to fulfilling their commitments. This structure allows for better decision-making and ensures that each task is carried out with care and precision.

Importance of Written Agreements

To avoid potential disputes in the future, it is critical to have a formal written partnership agreement. This document serves as the "bible" of the business, guiding decision-making, outlining responsibilities, and detailing how profits and losses will be shared. The agreement should cover essential points such as how major decisions will be made, how partners will resolve conflicts, and what the process will be for dissolving the business or exiting the partnership. When all partners agree on the terms and conditions outlined in the partnership agreement, it acts as a safeguard against misunderstandings and provides a reference point if disagreements arise. Having a solid agreement in place helps protect the interests of all involved and ensures the business stays on track.

Reflections on My Personal Experience in Partnership Business

Reflecting on my own experiences with partnership businesses, particularly the venture I started at my "Chawdi" (gathering place), has been a significant part of my growth as a businessman. Through these experiences, I've learned valuable lessons that have shaped my approach to partnerships and business in general.

Earlier in life, many relatives and even my mother consulted a Brahmin astrologer about my future, and I was told that "he will not succeed in a partnership business. He is too helpful to others but does not receive the same value in return. Therefore, he will never succeed in a partnership." At that stage of my life, I did not believe in such fortune-telling or horoscope predictions. However, looking back, I can see how these experiences, though disheartening, taught me valuable lessons about human nature, expectations, and business dynamics.

While I no longer place much stock in astrology, I must admit that the challenges I faced in partnerships confirmed some of the predictions made. Nevertheless, despite these early difficulties, I firmly believe that partnerships, particularly when the right people are involved, are more rewarding and productive than pursuing a business alone. Today, I am more committed than ever to growing my ventures through partnerships because of the shared success and collective growth that this model provides.

Why Partnership Works for Me

For me, the key to a successful partnership is choosing the right people—individuals who share mutual trust, respect, and a clear vision. When partners collaborate, support one another, and contribute their unique strengths to the business, the chances of success are significantly higher. I find that a partnership offers more fulfillment than a sole proprietorship because success is not only measured by financial gains but also by the satisfaction of fulfilling personal dreams while contributing to the success of others.

The feeling of shared accomplishment in a partnership, where all partners are equally invested in the growth of the business, is something that can't be replicated in a one-man operation. This sense of unity and collective achievement is a driving force behind my belief in partnerships as the most effective business model. When partners work together with sincerity, determination, and shared values, they can overcome any challenge and achieve greater success than they would individually.

The shared journey of building a business not only brings financial rewards but also creates a sense of community and collective responsibility, making the pursuit of success much more fulfilling. It is this sense of shared purpose that makes partnership businesses particularly powerful and rewarding.

Sharing My Personal Experience

Through my journey in partnership businesses, I have experienced both the highs and the lows. Each phase has imparted valuable lessons that I am eager to share with you. These lessons are not just theoretical; they are grounded in real-life experiences that have shaped my entrepreneurial path. As you embark on your own journey, whether you are just starting out or already running a business, I hope these insights will offer you guidance, helping you build stronger, more cohesive, and ultimately more successful partnerships.

Third Lesson: A Hard-Hitting Wake-Up Call

Fifteen years ago, as we began our work at the Chawdi, we were driven by the desire to empower farmers and women's self-help groups, aiming for their economic upliftment. At that time, social media distractions were not as prevalent as they are today, and the focus was on tangible work in the community. During this period, I crossed paths with two individuals from the Agriculture Office who were working on similar initiatives, and we started to build a connection. In addition to our social work, I was also exploring business ventures on the side, and it didn't take long for us to realize that our goals were aligned. We began having regular tea-time discussions, brainstorming ideas, and exploring how we could move forward together in partnership.

After seven or eight months of these discussions, one of us suggested forming a partnership, and all three of us agreed. This marked the start of a new business venture. We set up an office in a prime location in Nagar, where the three of us worked diligently to make informed, thoughtful decisions. Our business grew rapidly, and soon we had 24 franchises spread across Maharashtra. Through our efforts, we were able to assist farmers and create employment opportunities for young people. In Nagar, we organized self-help group exhibitions that drew attention and competed with some of the largest organizations in the industry for three consecutive years. The momentum was building, and everything seemed to be falling into place.

However, once the business became profitable, the dynamics within the partnership began to change. Despite the initial agreement regarding capital investment and time contributions, things didn't go as smoothly as expected. One partner, who had been given full signing authority for official responsibilities, manipulated the accounts, creating discrepancies in the financial records. This manipulation, despite the business having a large turnover, resulted in significant financial losses.

The partner in question, while holding official responsibility and a substantial role in the business, was also running a separate internal organization parallel to the main business. This created a conflict of interest, and the manipulation of the financials was done to benefit his personal interests. While I had contributed time, effort, and goodwill to the business for over four years, my smaller capital investment didn't shield me from the fallout. I suffered the consequences of these actions.

The second partner had made a larger capital investment, but due to his other job, he wasn't able to dedicate as much time to the business. This lack of time commitment led to him bearing the brunt of the financial burden, which caused him significant mental distress. Meanwhile, the third partner, who had been more passive in their involvement, managed to avoid the financial strain altogether. In the end, after a series of legal troubles and miscommunication, the third partner delivered a harsh but valuable lesson.

Lessons Learned:

- Trust, But Verify: This experience highlighted the importance of transparency and accountability in a partnership. Trust is essential, but it must be paired with oversight. Without proper checks and balances, even the most well-intentioned partners can veer off course.
- Clear Financial Management: Having a clear, shared understanding of financial practices and maintaining an impartial approach to handling money is crucial. This experience taught me that financial discrepancies can easily arise if one partner has too much control over the financial records.
- Know When to Act: Sometimes, partners may not fully disclose their actions or intentions. This situation taught me that it is important to act quickly when suspicions arise, especially when it comes to safeguarding the business's financial health. Ignoring red flags can lead to dire consequences.
- Division of Responsibilities: Clear boundaries and an equitable division of responsibilities are crucial in maintaining a successful partnership. If one partner is overburdened, it can lead to burnout, and if another partner is too passive, it can create resentment. A balanced partnership requires each partner to actively contribute according to their abilities.
- Legal Protections: Lastly, this experience underscored the importance of having a solid legal framework in place to protect all partners. A well-crafted partnership agreement and proper legal advice can prevent future misunderstandings and safeguard the business's integrity.

Through these trials, I learned valuable lessons that helped me grow not only as a businessperson but also as a partner. Partnerships can be a powerful way to grow a business, but they also require careful attention, transparency, and mutual respect to succeed. These lessons, though hard-won, continue to inform the way I approach partnerships to this day.

Capitalism and Socialist Ideals Don't Mix Well

The second significant lesson I learned, which deeply influenced the writing of this book, is about the intersection of capitalism and socialist ideals. This lesson came as a result of my personal experiences in business and how the pursuit of individual gain can often conflict with the values of collective welfare. At one point, I made the decision to leave my stable job to delve into socio-political research and election management, with the ambition of creating a home-based grocery delivery system as a sustainable source of income. This led to the formation of a business venture with several friends and colleagues, many of whom I had connected with via social media.

Over the next four years, the business grew, gaining recognition in the community. Our grocery delivery service became a trusted source for many during the pandemic, which allowed us to create a solid reputation. However, as is often the case in life, this success proved to be fleeting. Along with my marketing consultancy roles at BVG and later AVGC, my financial stability improved, and our grocery system further expanded into becoming a government supplier. We were thriving, helping young entrepreneurs and contributing to the economy. The number of partners in the business increased to eight, and over time, they, too, invested and contributed to its growth.

However, just as the business seemed poised for long-term success, everything began to unravel. At a crucial point, my daughter fell seriously ill, and I made the decision to take care of her at home. The business, which had been running smoothly, crumbled in my absence. The dreams I had worked so hard to build, all the structures I had put in place, seemed to vanish in an instant. It was a devastating blow, and I found myself questioning what had gone wrong. Yet, after deep reflection, I came to realize some important truths.

Even though some of the partners who had left the business had achieved material success—driving luxury cars and enjoying their financial prosperity—it was also heartening to see that many others, who had worked with me, had grown into successful entrepreneurs. They had broken free from poverty and achieved financial independence, something I take great pride in. Despite the setbacks and the loss of some partners, I found solace in knowing that I had been able to positively impact the lives of at least thirty individuals. These individuals, whom I had helped along the way, were now thriving in their own businesses. This, to me, was a true success.

The Unavoidable Question: Why Did They Leave?

What still bothers me, though, is why some of the people who had worked alongside me for years chose to leave. What went wrong? I spent countless hours reflecting on these questions, but in the end, I realized that the answers no longer matter. The individuals who left have moved on, and those who remain continue their own journeys, just as I have. There is no point in holding on to past grievances or questioning their decisions. The truth is, people come and go—some remain, and others take different paths. This is the way life unfolds.

The key lesson here is that no matter how much you help others, no one is obligated to stay by your side forever. Everyone has their own dreams, aspirations, and goals. They may share in the journey for a while, but eventually, they may feel the need to follow their own path. The people who left didn't abandon their success—they found their own way, and many of them are doing well now. This is simply a natural part of life, and over time, I've come to accept it. Life is not defined by the people who leave; it's defined by those who continue to walk alongside you, supporting and growing with you.

I've also had to leave some people behind at different stages of my life. That doesn't make them wrong or me right. It's simply how things evolve. The people who leave and the ones who stay are all part of the same journey. In both business and life, true success is not determined by the individuals who come and go but by how you continue to grow, evolve, and stay focused on your mission.

Today, I am still working with several like-minded individuals. We are all aligned in our values and professional goals, and that shared alignment is what makes the journey worthwhile. It's not about who's with you at any given moment, but about the collective strength you share with the people who remain committed to the same vision. This alignment, more than anything, is what has sustained me and will continue to drive my success in the future.

One of the most common mistakes entrepreneurs make is inviting someone into a partnership with the intention of uplifting them or helping them grow. Many believe that this goodwill will eventually lead to success. However, over time, they realize that this was the wrong decision. This isn't necessarily a fault of the individual, but rather a misstep in the selection process. Just as a business can fail when we fail to select the right customers, a partnership can fail when emotions, a sense of obligation, or a desire to "help" someone takes priority over practical business considerations.

In my case, I learned this lesson the hard way. It's important to ensure that both partners genuinely need each other and are prepared to work together in a manner that benefits the business. A partnership should be based on mutual need and readiness, not sentiment or goodwill alone. Even if partners enter the arrangement with good intentions, disagreements and conflicts are bound to arise. However, this does not mean that the partnership is destined to fail. Rather, it can offer valuable lessons and an opportunity to move forward stronger.

There will always be ups and downs, but as long as both parties remain committed to finding solutions, a way forward will eventually emerge.

Learning from the Example of Chatrapati Shivaji Maharaj

One of the most profound examples of leadership and collaboration comes from the life of Chatrapati Shivaji Maharaj. His leadership was instrumental in the establishment of the Maratha Empire. Shivaji Maharaj invested trust in his generals and soldiers—individuals like Tanhaaji Malusare, Baji Prabhu Deshpande, Kanhoji Jedhe, and Murarbaji—who supported him in building a strong foundation for Swarajya. Together, they created something remarkable. However, as history shows, not everyone who started with him remained by his side. Some of his allies eventually left, just as we might experience in our own businesses. When this happens, the message should always be: "May they prosper in their own way." It is important not to harbour resentment or blame others when they part ways. Instead, we should focus on the lesson and move forward.

This philosophy mirrors the approach that one of my partners, Mahadev Gawli, often emphasizes. He advises us to view life and business through a neutral lens—recognizing that every experience, good or bad, is a lesson to learn from. This mindset has been incredibly enriching, teaching me to focus on what really matters: not holding grudges but growing from each experience.

Internal Politics and the Need for Equal Leadership

Internal politics—particularly disputes over who is the "boss"—is a common issue in both political organizations and business ventures. It's inevitable that two or more people coming together to work will experience some rivalry or competition for leadership. The key, however, is to manage these struggles constructively and focus on the bigger picture. In any partnership, there should be no absolute "boss" or ruler. In today's world, no single individual can possess all the skills necessary to run an organization. Instead, leadership should rotate, with each partner taking charge in their area of expertise.

For example, in our partnership, Mahadev Gawli excels in procurement and operations, so he leads these aspects of the business. Sunil Zhagade, with his marketing skills, takes the lead in that domain. When it comes to technology, I step forward to manage it. In purchasing and supply, leadership is rotated between Mahadev Gawli and Vishal Vidhate, ensuring that everyone is involved and contributing according to their strengths. Even when I'm not physically present in the office, Maria Thorat and Madhuri step in to take charge as needed.

I've never felt the need to always be the "first" or "in charge." Those who insist on being the boss often end up isolating themselves from the group. From my experience, the best way to grow is by respecting and appreciating the talents and skills of others. Whether working with friends or business partners, I view them as the "leaders" when they excel in their specific areas. This attitude of mutual respect is crucial for success in any partnership.

Shivaji Maharaj's example of empowering others and focusing on collective strength serves as a guiding principle. It's not about one individual being in control but rather about each partner bringing their unique contributions to the table. This approach creates a collaborative, harmonious environment where everyone is valued and has the opportunity to lead in areas where they shine. When this mutual respect is fostered, success is not only achievable, but sustainable.

Respecting Skills and Leadership

This approach, where leadership is based on respect for skills and expertise, isn't just applicable in business—it extends across all aspects of life, whether social, political, or economic. Chatrapati Shivaji Maharaj's leadership exemplifies this by entrusting key responsibilities to those best suited for the task at hand. He understood when it was necessary to take charge and when to delegate authority. His leadership was never about control for the sake of control, but about ensuring that the right person was at the helm in every situation. This principle of flexible, skill-based leadership is just as important in business as it is in any sphere of society or governance.

By adopting this mindset, where leadership is fluid and shifts depending on the situation and the expertise needed, we not only ensure that the most informed and capable decisions are made but also foster a culture where everyone feels valued for their contributions. In any group or team, when individuals are recognized for their unique strengths and given the opportunity to lead when their expertise is required, the collective output becomes far more effective and efficient.

This approach is key to building strong, adaptable teams. It ensures that every person has the chance to step up when needed, while also enabling them to support others in areas where they are less experienced. This balance creates an environment of mutual respect and trust, where people are not only committed to their individual success but also to the success of the group as a whole.

The power of respecting and empowering others to lead when they possess the necessary skills is not confined to the workplace. In personal relationships, communities, and broader societal structures, this philosophy can help us navigate challenges and work together toward common goals. When everyone is given the space to lead in their own domain, we create a thriving, cooperative ecosystem—whether in business, politics, or social movements.

Ultimately, this principle of skill-based leadership cultivates an atmosphere of growth and learning, where people are motivated to continuously improve, share knowledge, and contribute to the collective progress. It is this respect for one another's abilities and leadership that lays the foundation for success, not just in business, but in every aspect of life.

Key Insights from My Business Journey:

- No Place for Blind Faith: In today's fast-paced and competitive marketplace, there's often a tendency to place blind faith in potential partners or external factors, believing they hold the key to success. While faith is important, it should not be blind or based on superstition, whether it's visiting a temple, wearing lucky charms, or relying on talismans for business success. True success in business is the result of hard work, diligent effort, and a commitment to teamwork. Success is not a magical solution that will simply appear through blind belief, but a practical result of persistence and strategy.

- No Place for Prejudices: Prejudices based on someone's community, caste, or religion can be destructive in both business and personal relationships. It's easy to make assumptions about trustworthiness or success based on these factors, but such assumptions are not only harmful but also unrealistic. A person's integrity or business capability is not determined by their background but by their skills, commitment, and work ethic. It's crucial to make business decisions based on practicality and mutual need, not on emotions or biased beliefs. Every person, irrespective of their background, has the potential to contribute to success if they are aligned with the goals of the partnership.

- Your Best Friend May Not Always Be Your Best Partner: Many entrepreneurs make the mistake of choosing close friends or family members as business partners, assuming that the personal bond will translate into a successful business collaboration. However, this can lead to emotional complications, misalignments, and conflicts. Large successful businesses often thrive because diverse minds come together to create something bigger than any one individual's vision. The key to a healthy partnership is balancing diverse opinions and leveraging each person's strengths. It's important to separate personal relationships from business dynamics and ensure that decisions are made based on the business's needs, not emotional ties or personal egos.

- Let Go of Ego Quickly: Ego, when balanced, can be a source of strength, boosting confidence and drive. However, when allowed to grow too large, it can become a destructive force in both business and personal life. An inflated ego often leads to conflicts, poor decision- making, and a lack of collaboration. To avoid this, it's important to regularly check your ego, stay open to new ideas, accept criticism, and let go of the need to always be "right." The most successful partnerships thrive when individuals are humble enough to learn, adapt, and work together toward shared goals.

- Maintain Practical Balance: Business relationships, like personal ones, should be grounded in practicality. Don't assume that a partner will stay forever out of gratitude or obligation. People's personal and professional circumstances evolve, and sometimes, business relationships may end or shift. This is a natural part of business life. While it's important to help others and have idealistic values, maintaining a practical, level-headed approach to business will prevent emotional turmoil. When a partnership ends, treat it as part of the natural course of business rather than a failure, and focus on moving forward with a pragmatic mindset.

- Don't Burden Others with Excessive Expectations: In business, it's easy to place high expectations on your partners, but this can lead to resentment and disappointment. While it's important to hold everyone accountable, setting unreasonable demands or expectations can create unnecessary stress. In my experience, it's essential to manage expectations fairly, communicate openly, and ensure that everyone contributes according to their strengths. Mistakes will inevitably happen, but the goal is to learn from them, grow, and avoid repeating them in the future. As an entrepreneur who didn't come from a family with a business legacy, I've learned that mistakes are an essential part of growth. What matters most is how we adapt and improve.

- Business Partnerships Are Critical: Choosing the right business partner is one of the most crucial decisions you can make in your entrepreneurial journey. Just like a good life partner can offer emotional support and stability, a good business partner provides the practical support needed to navigate challenges and grow the business. The right partner brings complementary skills, shares the load, and supports you in times of difficulty. A successful partnership can be the difference between thriving and struggling. I've shared these reflections from my own experiences in the hopes that they can help guide you as you build your own partnerships and business ventures. Embrace the lessons from experience, and you'll be well on your way to achieving success.

CHAPTER ELEVEN

Key Insights for Success in Business

Any business is not just a means to gain experience but a path towards success and financial growth. Therefore, when we choose a business, it is with the intent of creating a strategy that leads to prosperity. This strategy involves a clear understanding of the products and services offered, a research-driven approach, market observation, quality enhancement, marketing techniques, and customer engagement. A business is not just about selling goods or services; it requires a well-thought-out plan. With solid strategies in place, the likelihood of success increases significantly.

Clear Goals and Objectives:

The foundation of any successful business lies in having clear goals and objectives. It's essential to know exactly what you want to achieve, whether it's financial growth, market penetration, or product development. Your business goals act as a compass, guiding your decisions and actions. Whether you are focused on a specific niche or have a broader market in mind, your goals must be defined in measurable terms, and your strategy should be aligned with these goals. While it's natural that both strategies and goals might evolve over time, it's critical to have a defined direction. This allows you to pivot when necessary but ensures that you are always progressing toward a long-term vision. Knowing when to adjust your goals, and understanding the flexibility required, will help you stay on track, even as the business landscape changes.

Continuous Learning and Observation:

In the fast-paced world of business, standing still is not an option. Constant learning and keen observation are key to staying competitive. The business environment, consumer preferences, and technologies are always evolving, and staying informed about these changes will help you navigate challenges and seize new opportunities. Continuously seek knowledge through courses, industry events, and discussions with peers. At the same time, observe your surroundings carefully—understanding market trends, consumer behaviour, and industry shifts will help you anticipate change. Combining continuous learning with sharp observation equips you to adjust your strategies and remain relevant in an ever-changing world.

Focus on Quality and Innovation:

The quality of your products and services is the cornerstone of your business's reputation. Many new businesses thrive because they focus on offering high-quality products and services that meet customer needs. Over time, established businesses may lose their competitive edge due to complacency or failure to innovate. It's crucial to continually refine your offerings, maintaining high standards of quality and customer service. However, while offering top-notch quality is essential, be mindful of how you present your product or service. A balance is needed between innovation and practicality; over-promising or being overly idealistic in your approach can backfire. Keep a keen eye on customer needs and maintain a balance between offering excellent service and understanding when to introduce new features or products. Innovation should drive your business forward, but it should not come at the cost of customer satisfaction or overstretching your business resources.

Keep an Eye on Competitors:

Understanding what your competitors are doing is vital to staying ahead in business. While it's important not to obsess over them, keeping an eye on their strategies, offerings, and market positioning helps you identify areas of opportunity or threats. Competitors can often reveal industry trends, customer preferences, and even gaps in the market. By monitoring their actions, you can anticipate shifts in the market and adapt your strategy accordingly. However, it's important to remain focused on your own business and not get caught up in unnecessary personal conflicts with competitors. Healthy competition pushes you to be better, but engaging in petty disputes can derail your focus and lead to distractions. Focus on your business goals while using your knowledge of the competition to strengthen your position in the market.

Government Policies and Schemes:

Government policies and schemes can play a crucial role in the success or challenges your business faces. It's important to remain informed about any policy changes, as they can either benefit or negatively impact your business. For example, if you're in the renewable energy sector, schemes like Solar Gram or Suryaghar may offer incentives that promote your growth. On the other hand, if you are in the banking or financial services sector, changes like easier access to loans from government banks could lead to a shift in customer preferences, affecting private financial institutions. The key is to monitor these changes and find ways to leverage them to benefit your business. Staying updated on policies allows you to adjust your business strategies and make informed decisions that align with government initiatives.

Market Trends are the Highway to Growth:

Market trends are often the driving force behind a business's success. A prime example is the shift from burner phones to smartphones, which revolutionized the mobile phone industry. Companies like Nokia, BlackBerry, and Motorola, which once dominated the market, failed to recognize the importance of transitioning to smartphones, leading to their decline. In contrast, Apple's ability to adapt and innovate kept it at the forefront of the market. This example underscores the necessity of staying attuned to changing market needs and technological advancements. Without constant market research and a willingness to adapt, your business risks becoming obsolete. Successful businesses recognize emerging trends early on and pivot their offerings to meet evolving consumer demands, ensuring sustained growth.

Hard Work, Patience, and Consistency are Essential:

While hard work and persistence are essential for business success, they need to be complemented by the ability to seize opportunities when they arise. A holistic approach is required—one that combines patience with a proactive mindset. Take, for example, the story of Madhukar Shinde, who capitalized on the rise of Ayurveda by selling Ayurvedic powders at local fairs. His business grew as people began to appreciate the health benefits of his products. Similarly, his neighbour, who was initially struggling to sell books, identified an emerging market for Ayurvedic powders and began selling products from Shinde's stall. He eventually expanded his business into a successful brand called "Navi Jeevan." This story highlights the importance of observing market trends and responding to them.

However, simply identifying trends is not enough. A different entrepreneur who worked with Shinde initially saw success by supplying vegetables and Ayurvedic products to large companies in cities like Pune and Mumbai. However, when the quality of the products started slipping, the business suffered, and clients stopped purchasing. This example emphasizes that while market trends and opportunities are crucial, consistency in product quality is the real key to long-term success. Businesses that maintain high standards year after year are the ones that thrive in a competitive market. Quality, combined with the ability to adapt to new trends, forms the foundation of sustainable business growth.

The Power of Effective Strategy and Communication Skills:

Success in business goes beyond having the best products or services. One of the most powerful tools for achieving success is mastering effective communication. Communication is not just an exchange of words; it's an art that lays the foundation for building relationships, gaining trust, and achieving goals in any field.

Clear and Concise Speaking:

Before speaking, we should always take a moment to think. Speaking without first considering your words can lead to misunderstandings or careless statements. Effective communication begins with clarity. When conveying your business's objectives, strategies, and plans, they should be presented in a way that is easy to understand. A clear and straightforward approach increases the likelihood of getting the desired responses and fosters better understanding among colleagues, customers, or business partners. The key is to express yourself in a manner that ensures your message is both concise and clear, leaving little room for confusion.

Be an Active Listener:

Communication is not just about talking—listening plays a significant role too. Being an active listener means truly hearing what the other person is saying without interrupting, and understanding their point of view before responding. In business, this is particularly important. Whether interacting with customers, employees, or business partners, listening attentively allows you to respond more thoughtfully and effectively. It builds trust and creates a solid foundation for future decisions. It's also essential when you need to make strategic or technical changes, as understanding others' input and feedback helps inform these decisions and ensures they align with the needs and expectations of those involved.

Effective Use of Emotional Intelligence:

Effective communication isn't just about words—it's also about emotions, gestures, and body language. Emotional intelligence involves understanding and responding to the feelings and mental states of others in a way that fosters positive interaction. For example, if a customer is stressed or in a hurry, reacting in a rushed or dismissive way will only escalate the situation. Instead, a more empathetic and thoughtful response can transform the interaction, keeping it productive and positive. Mastering emotional intelligence helps in managing sensitive situations, resolving conflicts, and building stronger relationships with customers, employees, and partners. It's an essential tool for creating a harmonious business environment and ensuring long-term success.

Humility and Positivity Are Key:

Business, like life, is filled with challenges and setbacks. During tough times, it's easy to focus on the negatives, but it's far more productive to shift your attention toward the positive possibilities. Maintaining a positive outlook and focusing on solutions rather than problems can inspire your team and drive progress. Humility also plays an essential role. Leaders who exhibit humility—acknowledging their mistakes and showing respect for others—are more likely to foster an environment of trust and collaboration. This humility, combined with a positive approach, can motivate employees, win over customers, and build a reputation of integrity. In both internal business interactions and external ones with customers and the community, humility and positivity are vital for lasting success and meaningful relationships.

In essence, effective communication is at the heart of business success. It is not just about talking, but about listening, understanding emotions, staying humble, and keeping a positive perspective. These principles are foundational to building strong business relationships and navigating the challenges that inevitably arise in any business journey.

The Guidance of Saints in Business

The wisdom shared by saints throughout history offers invaluable guidance, not just for personal growth, but also for the world of business. One of the most influential figures in Marathi literature, philosophy, and the Bhakti tradition, Sant Tukaram Maharaj, provided profound insights into life, relationships, and business practices through his Abhangas (devotional hymns). His teachings, deeply rooted in truth, social values, and integrity, offer timeless lessons for anyone engaged in business or looking to lead a purposeful life.

Emphasizing Truth, Honesty, and Simplicity

Sant Tukaram Maharaj's teachings consistently advocated for truth, honesty, and simplicity as core values. He believed that these values were essential not only for personal life but also for building strong and trustworthy business practices. "Shed envy, maintain sweetness in the home; remain connected to truth, and chant the name of Vitthoba," he famously said. These words underscore the importance of fostering honest, transparent relationships in business. By doing so, businesses can build trust with their customers, employees, and partners, which is the foundation of long-term success. In a business world often driven by competition and profit, Sant Tukaram's call for simplicity and integrity remains a beacon of ethical business practices.

Humility and Continuous Learning

Sant Tukaram Maharaj also highlighted the importance of humility and continuous learning. He advised, "Learn the teachings of the saints, let pride stay away; never forget your roots, keep pure thoughts." This is an important reminder for businesses: no matter how successful one becomes, it's essential to remain open to learning and growing. Arrogance and a sense of superiority can block new opportunities and alienate others, but humility allows for continuous improvement and personal development. In business, this means staying receptive to feedback, learning from mistakes, and constantly evolving with changing markets and customer needs.

The Interconnectedness of Success and Social Well-being

Maharaj's teachings also stress the interconnectedness of individual progress with the welfare of society. He said, "When we connect all lives with love, we experience the divine blessings." This philosophy encourages business leaders to prioritize not just their financial success but also the well-being of their community and society at large. Leading businesses such as Tata, Amul, and Apple have adopted this principle, focusing on both profit and social responsibility. These companies understand that a business's success is intrinsically linked to the welfare of those it serves and the society it operates within. By nurturing these connections and building businesses based on mutual respect and trust, these companies have achieved enduring success.

Balancing Material Wealth and Spiritual Growth

One of the most important teachings from Sant Tukaram Maharaj is the balance between material wealth and spiritual growth. "Do not chase after wealth, for illusion is always harmful; keep it in your mind with caution," he warned. This teaching calls businesses to focus not just on financial gains but on sustainable, long-term growth. It reminds us that chasing wealth can sometimes lead to unethical practices or short-sighted decisions. Businesses should aim to create value, contribute to society, and operate with integrity, ensuring that financial success doesn't come at the expense of ethical principles or long-term sustainability.

Trust as the Backbone of Business

The importance of trust in business is another core principle of Sant Tukaram Maharaj's teachings. "Trust is the backbone of business, and it must always be maintained with honesty," he said. Trust is the most valuable asset a business can have, and it is built through consistent actions and transparent practices. When a business operates with honesty and integrity, it builds lasting relationships with customers, employees, and partners. This trust becomes the foundation for growth and resilience, allowing businesses to weather challenges and expand over time.

The Wisdom of Sant Dnyaneshwar Maharaj

Alongside Sant Tukaram, Sant Dnyaneshwar Maharaj's teachings also offer valuable insights into business. Known for laying the foundation of the Warkari tradition, Dnyaneshwar Maharaj emphasized values such as honesty, contentment, and hard work. "Every new day brings an opportunity, make a fresh attempt, and you will find a new path," he said, highlighting the importance of seizing opportunities and remaining optimistic. His wisdom encourages businesses to view each new day as a chance for growth, innovation, and improvement.

Dnyaneshwar Maharaj also emphasized patience and thoughtful decision-making, stating, "Decision-making should never be rushed, for a decision made with patience is always the right one." In business, making hasty decisions can lead to mistakes. Maharaj's advice to take the time to carefully consider options before acting is crucial for long-term success.

The True Wealth of Humility and Hard Work

Finally, Sant Dnyaneshwar Maharaj teaches that true wealth lies not in material possessions, but in humility and honest labour. "In simplicity, there is greatness, live without arrogance; humility is the true wealth, preserve it always," he said. He also highlighted the joy that comes from honest work: "In hard work lies joy, in work comes satisfaction, and in honesty comes respect." These teachings encourage business leaders to remain grounded, work diligently, and prioritize integrity in all their endeavours. True success, according to Maharaj, is measured not by the wealth one accumulates but by the satisfaction that comes from doing meaningful, honest work and treating others with respect.

Incorporating the teachings of these saints into business practices can help create a more ethical, sustainable, and socially responsible approach to entrepreneurship. Their guidance emphasizes that success is not just about profits but also about building relationships based on trust, humility, and service to the greater good. By following these principles, businesses can not only achieve financial success but also contribute positively to society and the lives of those they touch.

CHAPTER TWELVE

Let's Move Towards Progress Through Positivity, But...

We often hear that a positive mindset is the key to achieving success in life. While this is true to an extent, the idea that positivity alone guarantees success is misleading. Even with the most optimistic approach, can we accomplish everything we desire in the moment? The reality is no. If success were guaranteed simply by maintaining a positive attitude, books like this wouldn't be necessary, and failures would be mere anomalies. Yet, when we observe the world around us, it becomes evident that failure is far more common than success—both in the past and in today's world.

But does this mean that failure should deter us from striving for a good life, progress in business, and personal success? Absolutely not! Deep within every living being is an innate drive to improve and become the best version of themselves. Think about it: have you ever encountered anyone who consciously aims to be the worst? This intrinsic desire to progress, despite setbacks, is what defines us as humans.

Take, for instance, the stories of the founders of global brands like KFC and McDonald's. These individuals faced immense struggles, endured countless failures, and yet emerged as pioneers in their respective industries. What's most inspiring about their stories isn't the scale of their success or the fame of their brands but the resilience they demonstrated during their journeys. They confronted failure head-on, learned from it, and ultimately transformed their challenges into opportunities. Their paths were neither linear nor easy, and yet they persevered.

However, the inspiration drawn from such stories is often fleeting. Hearing their successes might motivate us momentarily, but to gain meaningful, lasting insights, we need to delve deeper. Understanding the phases of their failures, the thought processes that guided them through adversity, and the decisions they made in the face of uncertainty allows us to extract lessons that resonate with our own challenges. While we cannot replicate their exact experiences, the universal nature of struggles and the principles of resilience apply to every entrepreneur and individual seeking growth.

Learning from Struggles and Knowing What Not to Do

In life and business, the challenges we face are unique in their details but similar in their essence. That's why it's often said that knowing what not to do is just as important—if not more so—than knowing what to do. Avoiding common pitfalls and mistakes can often be the difference between success and failure. By understanding the missteps others have made and the lessons they've learned, we can chart a path that minimizes unnecessary obstacles.

A Parallel from Fiction: The Resilience of Tyrion Lannister

A striking example of resilience and determination can be found in the fictional world of *Game of Thrones*. Among the many complex characters vying for power and survival, Tyrion Lannister stands out. Known as "The Dwarf," Tyrion is a man who faces ridicule, rejection, and constant challenges, both internal and external. Yet, he navigates these crises with wit, courage, and an unwavering sense of self-worth.

Tyrion's journey is a powerful metaphor for life and business. Despite his physical limitations and societal prejudices, he uses his intelligence and resourcefulness to overcome adversity. His ability to face every challenge head-on and remain steadfast in his principles mirrors the journey of many entrepreneurs and professionals who encounter obstacles but refuse to give up. Tyrion teaches us that while circumstances may not always be in our favour, our mindset, adaptability, and willingness to fight for what we believe in can lead us to triumph.

Progress Requires Positivity, but Also Action

While positivity provides the foundation for resilience and perseverance, it is not enough on its own. Success requires a combination of optimism, strategic thinking, and consistent effort. It also requires the courage to face failure, learn from it, and move forward with renewed determination. True progress comes when we pair a positive outlook with thoughtful action, grounded in the lessons learned from our own experiences and the stories of those who came before us.

Ultimately, the path to success is not a straight road, but a winding journey filled with highs and lows. It is in navigating these twists and turns with determination, humility, and an open mind that we find not only success but also fulfillment and growth. So, let us embrace positivity—not as a guarantee of success but as a tool to face challenges—and couple it with a commitment to learn, adapt, and move forward.

The Resilience and Growth of Arya Stark

One of my favorite characters in *Game of Thrones* is Arya Stark, a young girl whose journey exemplifies resilience, adaptability, and the determination to achieve her goals. Arya's experiences teach her not only what to do but also what to avoid, shaping her into a character who discards the unnecessary and master's essential skills. What makes Arya special is her ability to evolve. She embraces change, adapts to challenges, and plans her actions based on her surroundings, all while staying true to her inner desires.

Arya's story, much like Tyrion's, resonates with life and business lessons. Both characters have contrasting approaches to life but share a willingness to adapt and survive. Their positive mindset toward achieving their goals is a common thread. They show us that while positivity is vital, it must be paired with adaptability and action to navigate the uncertainties of life effectively.

The Unpredictability of Success

Even with a positive attitude and a well-laid plan, success is never guaranteed. A simple example illustrates this: imagine a group of nine friends heading to Pune from Ahmednagar in two identical cars. Both cars set out on the same route and travel non-stop, yet they're unlikely to arrive at the same time. Why? Various factors come into play—driver skill, road conditions, traffic, unforeseen incidents like a puncture, or even a detour caused by an accident. Every decision made by the drivers and passengers influences the outcome.

Similarly, in life and business, the path to success is influenced by countless variables— some within our control and others governed by chance. Often, we switch lanes in traffic, hoping for a faster route, only to find that the other lane moves quicker. Whether we're delayed or make good time can feel like a matter of luck, leaving us frustrated or pleased based on circumstances outside our control. This randomness highlights the importance of patience, adaptability, and a balanced mindset.

The Role of Luck and Perspective in Success

This example of the car journey underscores the role of luck in determining outcomes. While skill, planning, and hard work are essential, we must acknowledge the influence of external factors beyond our control. Recognizing this can help us cultivate patience and maintain a positive perspective, even when things don't go as planned.

However, a positive approach doesn't mean blind optimism. It doesn't mean assuming that everything will fall into place simply because we believe it will. True positivity lies in staying grounded, prepared for challenges, and maintaining faith in our ability to overcome obstacles, even when the journey gets rough.

The Need for Patience and Understanding

As someone with a naturally quick temper, I've learned the importance of patience in personal and professional life. Patience, combined with a positive approach, doesn't mean blindly trusting in favourable outcomes or assuming that everyone and everything will align with our expectations. Names, for instance, may carry profound meanings but don't define the character of the person they belong to.

- A person named "Pandurang" may not embody the divine traits of Pandurang of Pandharpur.
- Someone called "Santosh" (contentment) might still struggle with inner peace.
- The name "Sagar" (ocean) might evoke vastness and depth, but its waves can still cause destruction.

This serves as a reminder that assumptions based on names, appearances, or affiliations can lead to misplaced expectations. Similarly, in business, we must look beyond surface labels like religion, caste, or nationality. We should embrace a broader perspective that views the world as one interconnected marketplace.

Beyond Biases in Business and Life

In today's socio-political climate, biases based on religion, caste, or nationality often dominate conversations. This narrow-minded approach can limit our vision and hinder progress. In business, as in life, success requires us to rise above these divisions and embrace a more inclusive perspective. Treating the world as our home, we must work with a mindset that transcends boundaries and unites people across cultures and ideologies.

By adopting such a holistic view, we not only create opportunities for personal growth but also contribute to building a more equitable and harmonious society. In this way, Arya Stark's adaptability and Tyrion Lannister's resourcefulness offer timeless lessons: life's path may be unpredictable, but with patience, adaptability, and a broader perspective, we can navigate it with resilience and purpose.

The Journey of Colonel Harland Sanders: Lessons in Resilience and Success

Colonel Harland Sanders, the founder of Kentucky Fried Chicken (KFC), is an enduring symbol of persistence and determination. His story is one of repeated failures and setbacks, yet he never wavered in his quest for success. Sanders wasn't someone who spent time simply theorizing or talking about business; instead, he dove into the challenges, learning and evolving through practical experience. His journey emphasizes a universal truth: there are no shortcuts to success. Success comes through unwavering effort, a positive outlook, and a commitment to continuous learning.

Key Lessons from Colonel Sanders' Life

1. Boost Self-Confidence and Abilities

Colonel Sanders' life underscores the importance of self-belief and skill enhancement. Instead of dwelling on negativity, focus on honing your abilities and building confidence. By improving your skills, you not only empower yourself but also inspire trust and cooperation among your team and peers. Confidence becomes contagious, fuelling collective progress.

2. Big Goals Are Not Mandatory

Running a business isn't about proving something to the world or invoking envy in others. Success doesn't need to conform to societal standards or comparisons. True success is measured by the satisfaction and fulfillment derived from your efforts, not by external accolades or recognition. Focus on your work, and let the outcomes speak for themselves.

3.Learn from Failure and Move Forward

Failure is a constant companion in the entrepreneurial journey and often provides the most valuable lessons. Colonel Sanders faced numerous setbacks but refused to be discouraged. When failure strikes, adopt a mindset of growth, learn from the experience, and press forward. Remember, "Victory lies beyond defeat." Failures are stepping stones that guide us closer to our ultimate goals.

4. Celebrate Small Successes

Every small success is a milestone worth celebrating. Great organizations are built on the collective efforts of dedicated individuals. Acknowledging and appreciating even minor achievements fosters motivation and strengthens team morale. At the same time, humility in success ensures that the journey remains rooted in purpose and gratitude.

5. Pair Determination with Action and Courage.

Determination without action is like a car without fuel—it won't move forward. Colonel Sanders demonstrated that courage and action must go hand in hand. Facing challenges head-on with courage while executing plans with precision creates a powerful synergy. Aligning your thoughts with deliberate actions brings your goals within reach, no matter how distant they may seem.

Colonel Sanders' Legacy

Colonel Sanders' story is a testament to the power of perseverance and the value of learning from setbacks. He turned his failures into stepping stones and showed the world that success is not a matter of luck but the outcome of relentless effort and a refusal to quit. Whether you are an entrepreneur, a professional, or someone striving for personal growth, the lessons from his life are universal and timeless.

Takeaway: Success is not about reaching a predefined destination but about the journey, the growth, and the impact you make along the way. Like Colonel Sanders, embrace the challenges, stay grounded in humility, and keep moving forward.

Decoding the Maze of Government Grant Schemes: A Guide for Entrepreneurs

Starting a business often requires significant financial investment, and government grant schemes can play a pivotal role in easing this burden. Central and state governments regularly introduce schemes designed to incentivize entrepreneurship and economic growth. While these schemes provide valuable financial assistance, they often come with challenges rooted in their design and implementation.

Many of these schemes are crafted by policymakers or bureaucrats with limited insight into the realities of business operations. This disconnect may lead to schemes that, while well- intentioned, may not align with the specific needs of every entrepreneur. Understanding these schemes thoroughly and determining their relevance to your venture is essential for making the most of these opportunities.

What Are Government Grant Schemes?

Government grant schemes, also known as subsidy schemes, are financial incentives aimed at supporting startups, small businesses, and economic development projects. They offer financial aid, reduced-interest loans, tax incentives, or other forms of support to eligible businesses.

However, the availability and nature of these schemes vary. They are often driven by political agendas, sector-specific priorities, or regional development goals. This means that the scheme you hope for may not exist, or its terms may not suit your project exactly.

How to Leverage Government Schemes Effectively

1. Understand Scheme Relevance

Start by researching schemes that align with your business idea. Different schemes cater to specific industries, demographics, or regional priorities. For instance, some might focus on technology startups, while others prioritize rural development or women-led businesses.

2. Analyse Rules and Requirements

Every scheme has its own set of eligibility criteria, rules, and terms. Study these carefully to ensure your business qualifies. Ignoring finer details may lead to rejection or complications during implementation.

3. Identify Challenges in Implementation

Even the best-designed schemes can face implementation hurdles. Delays, bureaucratic red tape, and complex application processes are common challenges. Assess whether the benefits outweigh the potential headaches.

4. Prepare a Comprehensive Business Plan

A solid business plan demonstrates your vision, objectives, and financial strategy. This not only strengthens your application but also builds trust with grant-approving authorities and financial institutions like banks.

5. Use Complementary Tools

Leverage other available resources like Udyam certificates, startup recognition programs, and collateral-free loans. Combining these tools with grant schemes can amplify the financial support for your venture.

Common Missteps and Misconceptions

- Misusing Grants: Many individuals start businesses solely to avail grants, without genuine intent or planning. This misuse contributes to a perception of fraudulence surrounding government schemes.
- Lack of Due Diligence: Jumping into a scheme without understanding its requirements often leads to wasted time and resources.
- Neglecting Feasibility: Just because a scheme offers financial aid doesn't mean it guarantees business success. The viability of the business model remains paramount.

A Responsible Approach to Grants

Government grant schemes are not a one-size-fits-all solution. They are tools meant to complement a robust business plan and genuine entrepreneurial efforts. If approached thoughtfully, these schemes can act as "booster doses," accelerating your journey toward success.

By conducting thorough research, planning meticulously, and adhering to ethical practices, entrepreneurs can harness the power of government schemes to fuel their ventures while contributing to economic growth and development.

Remember, grants and subsidies are enablers, not guarantees. Success ultimately depends on your vision, dedication, and ability to adapt to the ever-changing business landscape.

Advantages and Disadvantages of Government Grant Schemes

Government grant schemes are valuable tools for entrepreneurs, offering financial assistance and incentives to help establish and grow businesses. However, like any opportunity, they come with their own set of pros and cons. Here's a detailed overview:

Advantages of Government Grant Schemes

1. Access to Initial Capital

Many entrepreneurs struggle with raising the initial capital needed to launch a business. Government schemes can provide the much-needed financial foundation, especially for ideas that are still in the planning stage.

2. Support for Specific Sectors

Certain schemes target industries like agriculture, small-scale manufacturing, and women-led businesses. If your venture falls within these categories, the chances of receiving benefits increase significantly.

3. Reduced Financial Burden

Managing capital and loan repayments is often a significant challenge for new businesses. Grant schemes reduce this burden by offering subsidies, easy repayment options, and, in some cases, full financial assistance.

4. Encouragement for Innovation and Startups

With initiatives aimed at startups and MSMEs (Micro, Small, and Medium Enterprises), these schemes encourage innovation and entrepreneurship, fostering economic growth and job creation.

5. Boosting Underrepresented Entrepreneurs

Special schemes designed for women entrepreneurs, marginalized groups, or rural businesses help bring diversity to the entrepreneurial ecosystem by providing opportunities to underrepresented demographics.

Disadvantages of Government Grant Schemes

1. Complicated Application Processes

The paperwork and procedures involved in applying for government grants can be lengthy and confusing. Many entrepreneurs find the process so frustrating that they abandon their applications altogether.

2. Delayed Approvals and Inspections

Government schemes often involve extensive inspections and approvals, which can result in significant delays. This can hinder the timely launch or growth of a business.

3. Sector-Specific Limitations

Most schemes are tailored to specific industries or demographics. If your business does not align with these predefined categories, finding suitable financial assistance becomes challenging.

4. Political and Bureaucratic Challenges

Political interference and bureaucratic inefficiencies are common in grant schemes. Corruption, including demands for commissions or favouritism, often undermines the credibility of these programs.

5. Misallocation of Resources

Many schemes fail to reach genuinely needy entrepreneurs, as well-connected individuals or those without financial struggles often secure loans and subsidies. This leaves deserving applicants overlooked.

While government grant schemes provide significant advantages, such as financial support and reduced repayment burdens, they are not without their challenges. Entrepreneurs must navigate complex application processes and overcome bureaucratic hurdles to access these benefits. By being well-informed and prepared, one can maximize the advantages while minimizing the frustrations associated with these schemes. Ultimately, success depends on aligning your business goals with the available resources and leveraging them effectively.

Breaking the Maze of Government Subsidy Schemes: A Personal Experience

When I was just 16, the idea of becoming an entrepreneur planted itself in my mind, though it lacked clarity or direction at the time. I knew two essentials for starting a business: a solid idea and sufficient capital. To accumulate that capital, I took up various odd jobs. My academic journey, rooted in a science background, soon revealed my limitations—I was average at best, far from destined for a high-paying corporate job.

As I transitioned from FYBSc to commerce, the shift not only changed my academic path but also broadened my worldview. It exposed me to society and books, which became my lifelines. At the time, New Arts College in Ahmednagar (now Ahilyanagar) offered little in the way of real-world education. Many professors, under the guise of disciplinarians, resembled petty bullies more than mentors. Disillusioned by this lacklustre environment, I sought out alternative ways to learn.

Two places became my sanctuaries: Google and the public library near the Shivaji Maharaj statue. From morning to evening, I immersed myself in knowledge, piecing together bits of wisdom about the world and, more importantly, the workings of the entrepreneurial landscape. It was during one of these forays that I stumbled upon the District Industries Centre (DIC), which introduced me to government subsidy schemes—a beacon of hope for someone seeking financial aid to start a business.

Determined, I began visiting the DIC and employment exchange offices regularly, juggling thoughts of entrepreneurship with aspirations for MPSC and UPSC exams. At one point, after missing my chance at NDA, I even considered Class 1 officer exams. Yet, the pull of entrepreneurship remained strong, never fading into the background.

The DIC in Ahmednagar was a peculiar place. I remember a Maruti 800 parked outside, proudly bearing the name of a local politician, and a stout man named Nana who seemed to run the show. Nana was our self-proclaimed guide to the labyrinth of government offices. Under his "mentorship," my friends and I spent over a year navigating this convoluted system, only to be deceived. Nana swindled ₹50,000 from us—a sum painfully sourced by pawning my mother's jewellery at the Nagar Urban Bank. Promising us subsidies, he strung us along until it became clear we had been conned.

Simultaneously, my efforts to secure loans from banks met with repeated rejection. Frustrated and disheartened, I turned my focus back to education, preparing for government exams like MPSC. Even after reaching the PSI interview stage, I realized that a government job was not my calling. That chapter closed, but it led me to journalism—a profession that ultimately laid the foundation for my entrepreneurial journey.

For the next 20 years, I avoided government schemes and bank loans altogether, relying instead on private loans to kickstart my ventures. By using these funds wisely and methodically, I gradually built my creditworthiness. Over time, the same banks and government departments that once turned me away began offering me loans and subsidies. By then, however, I had learned how to navigate these systems effectively—a skill honed through years of trial and error.

Today, I look back at this journey with a sense of clarity. My initial failures with government schemes taught me resilience, adaptability, and the value of self-reliance. While the road was arduous and littered with setbacks, those experiences shaped my approach to entrepreneurship.

This story of grappling with subsidy schemes ends here, though the lessons learned might inspire an entirely separate book someday. For now, I leave this saga with a sense of closure, ready to share what I've learned with those embarking on similar journeys.

And then, a young 65-Year-Old Man Built a World-Famous Brand

The story of Harland Sanders is a true inspiration—an example of how persistence and reinvention can turn failure into success. In our society, the common belief is that once a person crosses 60, they are expected to retire. But Sanders defied this notion and proved that age is no barrier to chasing dreams. At 65, when most people give up on ambitions, he laid the foundation for a business model that would change the global fast-food industry.

The secret to his success lay in his unique fried chicken recipe and the franchising model he built around it. Many people possess great recipes, but lack marketing skills or fail to expand beyond their local area. Consequently, talented homegrown businesses often fade away due to their inability to scale.

A similar situation can be observed in the small town of Rajur in Akole Taluka, Ahmednagar. Located near Bhandardara Dam, this quaint village is known for its famous peda (sweet). Travelers who visit the region always return with a box of Rajur's pedas. Many shops now sell these sweets along the roadside, and their taste and color remain identical. However, within the old marketplace, there are traditional shops that have been making pedas for generations—offering a pure, authentic taste, without artificial colors or additives.

Despite having superior products, these traditional shops struggle with customer engagement. The shopkeepers, sitting at their cash counters with an air of arrogance, fail to welcome customers with a smile or treat them with respect. They make no effort to compete with newer businesses or adapt to market trends. Consequently, modern competitors who focus on aggressive marketing and visually appealing packaging have captured a significant share of the market.

This is where KFC's story comes in—a brand that did not fade away but instead evolved and expanded globally.

From a Small Roadside Stall to a Global Brand: The Story of KFC

In the 1930s, Harland Sanders set up a small roadside eatery next to a gas station in Kentucky. His goal was simple: serve travelers with delicious, home-style meals that would keep them coming back. Among his dishes, his unique recipe for fried chicken became a hit, making him locally famous.

As time passed, he expanded and opened a proper restaurant, enjoying steady business growth. However, in 1955, things took a drastic turn when a new highway bypass was constructed, diverting traffic away from his location. His once-thriving restaurant faced a sudden collapse.

In today's world, we see a similar trend. New highways, bypass roads, and urban development projects have caused many businesses to relocate or shut down. Some entrepreneurs adapt and find new opportunities, while others fail to recover.

Sanders, despite being 65 years old and financially ruined, refused to accept defeat. Instead of lamenting his losses, he decided to leverage what he had left—his recipe.

He took an unconventional approach, something that most people would have dismissed as unrealistic. If he no longer had a restaurant, why not sell his special recipe instead?

Thus began his journey of franchising.

With his secret blend of herbs and spices, he traveled across America, pitching his recipe to restaurant owners, offering them the opportunity to serve his chicken under a franchise model. The process was grueling—he received over 1,009 rejections.

But he did not give up.

Persistence paid off when one restaurant finally agreed, marking the birth of Kentucky Fried Chicken (KFC).

Today, KFC franchises are spread across the world, including in small Indian towns. This monumental success was built on consistency, resilience, and the ability to adapt to changing circumstances.

Understanding Business Dynamics: The Right Strategy for the Right Canvas

Last month, while chatting with Dr. Prafull Gadge and Umesh Bhosale at a chai shop in Kedgaon, we discussed the rise and fall of businesses. One analogy that emerged from our discussion was that of canvas and brushes—how businesses, like paintings, need the right tools and scale to succeed.

Consider brands like Café Coffee Day (CCD), Yevale Tea, and Amruttulya franchises—many of them have expanded rapidly, while others have struggled or shut down. Similarly, the Big Bazaar retail chain once dominated the market, but today, it no longer exists. Meanwhile, brands like Onida, Akai, Sharp, Nokia, HTC, and BlackBerry once led their industries but failed to evolve, causing them to disappear from the market.

A major reason behind such failures is a mismatch between the business size, strategy, and adaptability.

A painter, when working on a small canvas, doesn't need large brushes. Similarly, a large canvas requires appropriately sized brushes and an artistic vision to fill the space effectively. The same applies to businesses—without the right tools and approach, even great ideas fail to materialize.

I know someone who was instrumental in building a billion-dollar company but struggled to run his own business. His failure wasn't due to a lack of skill, but because he couldn't match his strategy with the scale of his business.

Every enterprise demands a unique approach. Recognizing the size, scope, and potential of a business is crucial to determining its success or failure.

A Parallel to the Game of Thrones: Survival of the Most Strategic

Looking back at history, we see a recurring cycle of rise and fall—empires, businesses, and even individual success stories follow the same pattern. Many powerful dynasties rose and fell, either due to poor leadership, complacency, or failure to adapt.

This reminds me of Game of Thrones, a show that captivated audiences worldwide. Some found flaws in the storytelling, but the series brilliantly portrayed how success depends not just on brute strength but also on intelligence, adaptability, and strategy.

One of my favorite characters from the series is Tyrion Lannister. Unlike others who fought for power, Tyrion understood the importance of strategy, alliances, and information. He was neither the strongest nor the most privileged, but his wit and wisdom allowed him to survive the harshest challenges.

Businesses operate in the same way. The market rewards those who think ahead, anticipate risks, and make informed decisions.

Tyrion once said, *"A mind needs books like a sword needs a whetstone."* Similarly, in business, knowledge and adaptability are as crucial as capital and investment.

The Battle of Blackwater was one of his finest moments. With limited resources, he used strategy over brute force, deploying wildfire to destroy an overwhelmingly powerful fleet. This same principle applies in business—small but strategic moves can defeat much larger competitors.

Effective negotiation and resource management are key to success, whether in business or warfare. In the series, Tyrion used his intellect to build alliances, manage conflicts, and ensure survival.

His ability to anticipate challenges, adapt to situations, and stay ahead of his enemies is exactly what makes businesses thrive.

I have often said, "Data is gold." Tyrion understood this too—he maintained a network of spies and informants to stay ahead of the game.

A successful business operates on similar principles—strong leadership, market awareness, flexibility, and the ability to make smart decisions at the right time.

The lesson remains the same: whether in business, history, or politics, survival belongs to those who evolve, learn, and strategize.

CHAPTER THIRTEEN

Social Approach and Image Building: A Balanced Perspective

A social approach plays a pivotal role in shaping the success of a business. However, it requires a thoughtful strategy and careful execution. It does not mean dedicating oneself entirely to social service but involves deliberate efforts to build a positive image of your business and brand within society. This approach fosters trust and credibility, which, in turn, translates into tangible benefits for the business.

Prominent Indian business groups such as Tata, Birla, Adani, Reliance, Wipro, Infosys, and others exemplify this balanced approach. While their primary goal remains business growth and profit, they actively contribute to social, educational, and scientific initiatives. These contributions have earned them immense respect and trust on both national and global scales.

Networking Through Social Initiatives

One of the most effective ways to enhance a brand's reputation is through networking, which can be significantly bolstered by engaging in social causes. Supporting community welfare projects positions the company as ethical, responsible, and caring. This not only strengthens relationships with customers but also helps the brand stand out in a competitive market.

However, this approach is a double-edged sword. Some entrepreneurs, especially those new to financial success, might lose focus and shift their priorities toward flaunting their wealth or building political connections. Adopting titles like "Sheth" (businessman) or "Sahab" (boss) and seeking social status through superficial gestures can detract from genuine social impact. This often leads to stagnation, as the original goal of meaningful outreach gets overshadowed by personal ambitions.

Defining Clear Goals

Before venturing into social initiatives or politics, it is crucial for an entrepreneur to clearly define their primary goals. Ask yourself:

- Is the focus on building and growing your business?
- Is the aim to serve the community through social work?
- Or is it to pursue political aspirations?

While it is possible to blend all three, clarity about the primary goal is essential to avoid dilution of effort and resources.

A Lesson in Overreach

A real-life example illustrates the consequences of an ill-planned social approach. A once-struggling entrepreneur who became a successful builder decided to "develop" his native village. He initiated ambitious projects such as constructing temples, digitizing schools, and providing services that were beyond the community's immediate needs.

While his intentions seemed noble, the local community, especially the youth, perceived these efforts as disconnected from their actual challenges. Some even speculated that his actions were driven by personal gain or corruption. Instead of appreciation, his well-meaning actions resulted in criticism, eroding the positive image he had worked so hard to build.

This story underscores the importance of understanding community needs before embarking on social initiatives. Social service efforts should align with what the community genuinely requires and is ready to embrace.

Key Takeaways for a Balanced Social Approach

1. Authenticity Matters: Ensure that social initiatives stem from genuine intent rather than a desire for recognition or political gain.

2. Community-Centric Planning: Study and address the actual needs of the community instead of imposing grand projects.
3. Clarity of Purpose: Clearly define the primary goal—whether it is business growth, social service, or politics—and prioritize accordingly.
4. Avoid Overcommitment: Social efforts should complement business objectives, not overshadow or detract from them.
5. Long-Term Trust Building: A carefully planned social approach builds lasting trust and credibility, ensuring sustainable benefits for both the community and the business.

By balancing business growth with meaningful social contributions, entrepreneurs can create a legacy of trust, respect, and enduring success. However, the key lies in thoughtful planning, sincerity, and alignment with the community's real needs.

The Role of Social Approach and Image Building in Business Success

For a business to thrive, several elements must come together, and one of the most critical is a social approach. This involves not just delivering services and selling products but actively engaging with the community to build meaningful relationships. A well-thought-out social perspective facilitates financial growth and strengthens credibility, making your business a trusted name in the community.

Understanding the Social Approach

A social approach cannot be superficial or imposed. It must evolve naturally through study, observation, and experience. A strategic yet genuine social perspective allows for organic business growth and stronger connections. Here are some practical ways to apply this approach:

1. Networking Opportunities: Regularly meet professionals from various fields by attending business meetings, consumer meets, and social networking events.
2. Engagement Through Initiatives: Organize and participate in social initiatives, as these enhance trust and increase visibility for your business.

3. Customer Connection: Foster direct communication with customers and every part of your distribution network. Hosting seminars, events, and feedback sessions helps maintain this vital connection.

Social Media: A Modern Tool for Engagement

In today's digital era, leveraging social media is no longer optional but essential. Platforms like Facebook, Instagram, LinkedIn, and Twitter enable businesses to maintain consistent communication with their audience. This includes:

- Sharing product and service updates.
- Quickly responding to customer queries and feedback.
- Building a narrative that resonates with your audience.

Many successful agricultural businesses, such as Biome, Sugar Master, and The Farm, are excellent examples of leveraging social platforms to establish trust and grow their client base. They maintain strong connections with farmers and clients through transparency, regular updates, and proactive communication.

Building a Strong Team

A business's success heavily depends on its team dynamics. A motivated and happy team leads to smoother operations and higher customer satisfaction. Here's how you can nurture your team:

- Open Communication: Regularly engage with employees, listen to their ideas, and value their feedback.
- Respect and Recognition: Treat team members with respect and acknowledge their contributions.
- Ethical Environment: Lead by example with ethical actions and inspire trust through fairness and transparency.

When employees feel valued and respected, they are more productive, and this positively impacts the business's overall growth and customer relations.

The Power of Image Building

Beyond the social approach, a business's image is a crucial factor in its success. Image building refers to shaping the perception of your business, brand, or self in the public's mind. It goes beyond having good products—it's about how you're viewed by your customers, employees, and the broader community.

Key elements of image building include:

1. Consistency in Behaviour and Actions: Your daily interactions and decisions should reflect your business's core values.
2. Lifestyle and Presentation: How you present yourself—your appearance, language, and demeanour—also plays a role in forming a positive image.
3. Inspiring Trust: Uphold honesty and reliability in all dealings to inspire long-term trust.

A well-maintained image acts as a force multiplier, boosting your brand's reputation and ensuring customer loyalty.

Combining a strong social approach with deliberate image-building efforts creates a solid foundation for business success. Engaging with the community, leveraging digital tools, nurturing team relationships, and maintaining an inspiring personal and professional image are vital. When these elements are in harmony, businesses not only grow financially but also leave a lasting impact on their communities.

Proper Reading Cultivates a Positive Outlook

The saying "Read and you will grow" is more than just a phrase—it encapsulates a powerful truth. Reading expands our horizons, enhances our understanding, and shapes our perspectives. However, what we read and whose works we choose to engage with are equally critical.

In a diverse country like India, where freedom of expression thrives, the publishing world is vast and varied. While this is a strength, it also means that some books focus on sensationalism or biased narratives rather than truth and constructive ideas. For example, figures like Jawaharlal Nehru and Mahatma Gandhi, pivotal in shaping modern India, are often subjects of works that emphasize their mistakes rather than their monumental contributions. Mahatma Gandhi himself openly discussed his flaws in *My Experiments with Truth*, yet many authors disproportionately highlight such aspects, distorting public perception.

This highlights the importance of selective reading. Being critical and intentional about our reading choices ensures that the information we consume builds us up rather than confuses or misleads us.

The Need for Discerning Reading Habits

In today's fast-paced world, where hundreds of books are published globally each day, it's impossible to read everything. Attempting to do so can leave us overwhelmed and lead to superficial knowledge. Instead, the key lies in prioritizing quality over quantity:

- Choose books by credible authors and publishers. Focus on works that offer professional insights, socio-political clarity, and constructive learning.
- Stay updated on current affairs and innovations. Daily newspapers, reputable magazines, and professional blogs are excellent resources.
- Diversify your reading. Biographies, financial guides, and books on business, marketing, and investment are essential for personal and professional growth.

Exploring Digital Resources for Continuous Learning

The digital age has transformed the way we access and consume information. Here are some powerful tools to broaden your knowledge base:

Blogs

Professional blogs often feature expert advice, real-life experiences, and practical solutions. Reading blogs written by industry leaders offers direct, actionable insights.

Video Blogs (Vlogs) and Podcasts

With the rise of platforms like YouTube, Spotify, and Audible, accessing high-quality educational content has never been easier. Popular YouTubers like Dhruv Rathee and Vikas Divyakirti share in-depth analyses and knowledge, inspiring new ideas and positive energy. Podcasts are equally enriching, offering diverse topics ranging from business and personal development to mindfulness and innovation.

Audio Platforms

Apps like Storytel, Snowell, Pocket FM, and Kukufm provide access to audiobooks, making it easy to learn on the go. They are perfect for multitasking professionals who want to maximize their time.

Interactive Tools

Platforms like Google, Blogger, and ChatGPT are invaluable for quick learning and idea exploration. These tools allow you to gain insights, clarify doubts, and stay updated with global trends at your convenience.

Benefits of Reading for Professionals

For business leaders and professionals, cultivating a reading habit goes beyond acquiring knowledge—it enhances critical thinking and decision-making skills. Reading provides:

- Clarity in thinking: Books and articles offer diverse viewpoints that sharpen analytical abilities.
- Inspiration: Learning about success stories and innovative ideas sparks creativity.
- Skill development: Specialized literature in finance, marketing, and management strengthens professional capabilities.
- Perspective building: Understanding socio-political dynamics fosters well-rounded decision-making.

In a world brimming with information, proper reading is not just a habit—it's a superpower. Whether through traditional books or digital platforms, the content we consume has the potential to shape our minds, decisions, and ultimately our lives. By choosing wisely and embracing a balanced mix of reading and digital learning, professionals can cultivate not only a positive outlook but also a competitive edge in their fields.

Experience is Our True Guru

Success in business, much like life, is built on the foundation of experience. While theoretical knowledge and advice from others play their part, nothing compares to the depth of understanding gained through personal encounters and challenges. Experience is the teacher that shapes us, guides us, and helps us navigate the complexities of both life and business.

Mistakes: The Stepping Stones to Growth

Every entrepreneur, no matter how successful, has made mistakes. These errors are not setbacks but opportunities to learn, adapt, and grow. Mistakes are inevitable, especially in the early stages of a business. I, like countless others, have made many missteps along the way. However, what distinguishes successful entrepreneurs is their ability to learn from these experiences and use the lessons as stepping stones toward success.

Just as life constantly evolves, so does business. Change is inevitable, and mistakes are an inherent part of the journey. The key lies in embracing them as learning opportunities and using the wisdom gained to refine strategies and make informed decisions.

The Power of Reflection

Every challenge and mistake holds a lesson waiting to be uncovered. Taking the time to reflect on experiences allows us to extract valuable insights. This process builds self- confidence and enhances our decision-making abilities.

With time, experience equips us to anticipate challenges, generate innovative ideas, and craft effective business strategies. It serves as a lens through which we can foresee opportunities and prepare for future hurdles.

The Role of Experimentation

Business success often stems from a willingness to experiment and take risks. Fear of failure or making mistakes can be a significant barrier, but without trying new approaches, growth becomes stagnant. Mistakes are the fertile ground where innovation and long-term vision take root.

Rather than focusing solely on immediate gains, experience teaches us patience and cultivates a mindset geared toward sustainable success. This perspective helps in building businesses that not only endure but thrive over time.

Learning from Others' Experiences

While personal experience is invaluable, learning from the journeys of others can provide shortcuts to wisdom. Studying the stories of successful entrepreneurs, understanding their mistakes, and drawing lessons from their paths can help us avoid common pitfalls and make better decisions.

This dual approach—gaining personal experience while leveraging the insights of others—creates a well-rounded foundation for entrepreneurial success.

Key Takeaways

1. Embrace Mistakes: See them as opportunities for growth rather than failures.
2. Reflect and Learn: Analyse experiences to gain insights and build confidence.
3. Experiment and Innovate: Take calculated risks to discover new opportunities.
4. Cultivate Patience: Focus on long-term sustainability over immediate gains.
5. Learn from Others: Study the journeys of successful entrepreneurs for inspiration and guidance.

Experience is the ultimate guru, guiding us through the uncertainties of business and life. By embracing mistakes, reflecting on lessons, and continuously learning—both from ourselves and others—we can build resilience, sharpen our vision, and pave the way for lasting success.

Investment Awareness is the Lifeblood of Successful Business

When we think about investment, the first thing that usually comes to mind is money. However, in the context of business, investment encompasses much more than just financial contributions. It also involves the time we dedicate, the skills we acquire, the knowledge we gain, and the resources we allocate for research and development. Every action taken with the intention of growth is an investment. To achieve success in any business, the most crucial investment is the one you make in yourself.

The First Investment: In Yourself

Business begins in the mind. As my friend Kishore Raktate once said, "Business starts in the mind, and only then does it take shape and expand." To initiate any venture, it's essential to foster positive thoughts and, more importantly, to have the confidence to take that first step. This confidence is not something that can be purchased—it is an investment in self- belief, a product of personal growth and reflection. The key is to invest in your own development: nurturing a growth mindset and cultivating the belief that you can turn your vision into reality.

Investing in Business and Relationships

Once you've made the initial investment in yourself, the next step is investing in your business. This includes not only financial resources but also time and energy spent on team building and forging relationships with trustworthy business partners, colleagues, and vendors. A successful business relies on honesty and commitment, qualities that cannot be bought. Genuine relationships, built on trust and mutual respect, require continuous investment.

This investment involves nurturing professional relationships, understanding the needs of your partners, and working together toward common goals. Success in business is not just about making money; it's about creating a network of committed individuals who believe in your vision and are willing to invest in it alongside you.

Continuous Investment in Learning and Growth

The process of investing in yourself is ongoing. In business, continuous learning and development are key to staying competitive. Investing in education, acquiring new skills, and gaining experience are essential to developing the leadership qualities that drive business success. This includes everything from mastering business management skills to improving financial literacy. Your ability to make informed decisions and seize opportunities depends on the knowledge you gather over time.

Remaining alert and aware of industry trends and emerging opportunities is critical. Success is rarely guaranteed, and while some investments may not yield immediate returns, perseverance and ongoing learning are essential. In fact, it's through staying vigilant and adaptable that you can recognize new opportunities and maximize the returns on your investments.

Staying Attuned to Changes and Opportunities

In today's fast-paced business world, technology plays a transformative role. Industries across the globe are continually evolving, and businesses that fail to keep up with technological advances risk being left behind. Investing in new technologies, understanding digital marketing, embracing e-commerce, and effectively using social media are now vital to any business strategy.

Keeping track of these changes requires constant effort and investment in research and development. For instance, businesses that neglect technological advancements or fail to embrace digital platforms often find themselves at a disadvantage. Even billion-dollar companies have faltered due to their inability to adapt to changing technologies and consumer behaviour.

Investment in Your Team

Your team is the backbone of your business. Investing in your employees' growth, training, and well-being is just as important as any other investment. A strong, well-trained team contributes to the smooth functioning of your business and drives its long-term success. Investing in your team creates a motivated, skilled workforce capable of meeting challenges and seizing new opportunities.

This investment should also extend to financial planning. Maintaining a clear, transparent financial strategy and regularly updating your balance sheet are essential to ensuring the financial health of your business. Every investment carries risk, but with sound financial planning, you can mitigate these risks and make well-informed decisions that will sustain and grow your business.

Customer Satisfaction: An Ongoing Investment

Another crucial investment is in customer satisfaction. Happy customers are loyal customers, and ensuring their satisfaction should be at the heart of your business strategy. Whether through product quality, excellent customer service, or creating a positive experience, consistently investing in customer relationships helps build a solid reputation and encourages repeat business.

To achieve long-term growth, businesses must look beyond short-term profits and focus on the future. This means making decisions with a long-term perspective, carefully considering the potential impact of every investment, and staying open to new opportunities as they arise.

Key Takeaways:

1. Invest in Yourself: Your mindset, confidence, and skills form the foundation of your success.
2. Build Strong Relationships: Invest in genuine, long-lasting partnerships with employees, colleagues, and vendors.
3. Commit to Continuous Learning: Stay informed and continuously improve your business acumen to adapt to changes and seize opportunities.
4. Embrace Technology: Stay updated on technological trends and integrate them into your business practices.
5. Invest in Your Team: Provide training, development, and a positive work environment to foster growth and efficiency.
6. Customer Satisfaction is Key: Ensure your customers are happy and loyal through consistent, quality service.
7. Think Long-Term: Focus on sustainable growth and always consider the future when making business decisions.

Investment is much more than just a financial endeavour—it encompasses time, knowledge, relationships, and resources. Whether it's investing in yourself, your team, or new technologies, a strategic approach to investment is crucial for long-term business success. By continually investing in these areas, you lay a solid foundation for growth, innovation, and sustainability, ensuring that your business remains competitive and thrives in an ever- changing market.

Difference Between Business and Investment

The terms "business" and "investment" are often used interchangeably, but they represent distinct concepts with different objectives, strategies, and outcomes. While both play essential roles in wealth creation and economic growth, it's important to understand the fundamental differences between them.

Business: A Holistic Approach

A business is an entity or organization engaged in commercial, industrial, or professional activities with the primary goal of generating profits through the sale of goods or services. Starting and running a business involves a significant amount of time, effort, creativity, and resource management. The business owner or entrepreneur invests not only financial capital but also personal time, energy, and skills into developing products or services, building a team, and ensuring the organization's growth.

In the case of industrialists like Tata, Reliance, Adani, and Jindal, their approach is rooted in entrepreneurship. These individuals are not merely investing money; they are using their time, expertise, and other resources to build and grow companies. Their success comes from active involvement in the day-to-day operations of the business, strategic decision-making, and long-term planning. They focus on creating value through innovation, scalability, and efficient management of their businesses.

Investment: A Financial Strategy

Investment, on the other hand, typically refers to allocating money or capital into assets with the expectation of generating a return over time. This can include a variety of sectors such as the stock market, real estate, bonds, mutual funds, or emerging assets like cryptocurrencies. The primary objective of investment is to grow wealth by leveraging market opportunities without necessarily being actively involved in the operational aspects of a business.

Warren Buffet, Rakesh Jhunjhunwala, and other renowned investors focus on putting money into assets that will yield financial returns. Unlike entrepreneurs, they don't actively manage the operations of the businesses they invest in; rather, they make strategic decisions based on financial analysis, market trends, and risk assessment. Their wealth grows by holding investments over time and benefiting from the appreciation in the value of assets.

Key Differences Between Business and Investment

1. Objectives:

    - Business: The goal is to create and deliver products or services, manage operations, and generate revenue. Entrepreneurs are focused on building a sustainable business model that creates value in the long run.
    - Investment: The goal is to grow wealth by putting money into assets that are expected to increase in value. Investors seek financial returns on their investments, typically without engaging in day-to-day management.

2. Methodology:

    - Business: Involves active participation in operations, innovation, marketing, customer service, and team management. Entrepreneurs are deeply involved in the decision-making and execution of strategies.
    - Investment: Involves placing capital into financial instruments or assets, monitoring them for growth, and possibly adjusting the portfolio. Investors usually rely on market analysis and expert advice to guide their decisions.

4. Risk and Control:

    - Business: Entrepreneurs assume higher operational risks but have control over the direction of their company. They face challenges related to market competition, operations, and customer acquisition but also have the potential for greater rewards if their business succeeds.

- Investment: Investors generally face financial risks but have less control over the business or asset. Their risk is typically tied to market volatility or the performance of individual assets. While there's potential for high returns, the investor is not directly involved in managing the underlying business.

5. Time Commitment:

- Business: Starting and running a business requires significant time and effort. Entrepreneurs are often dedicated to managing their company, overseeing daily operations, and making strategic decisions.
- Investment: Investment can be passive, requiring less time and active involvement once the capital is placed. While investors may occasionally need to monitor their portfolio or adjust their investments, they do not spend as much time in direct management of their assets.

Which Path to Choose?

While both business and investment are valid routes to wealth creation, choosing the right path depends on individual goals, interests, and resources. Here are some key considerations:

- Entrepreneurs who are passionate about creating and running businesses, solving problems, and building teams should pursue the path of business. Their focus will be on growing a company and taking a hands-on role in operations.
- Investors who are more interested in financial strategies and prefer less involvement in day-to-day operations may opt to invest their money in various assets. Investors can benefit from market trends, asset appreciation, and diversification without being actively engaged in business management.

It's not necessarily about one being better than the other—it's about aligning your approach with your personal strengths, interests, and goals. Both entrepreneurship and investing have the potential for significant financial gain, but they require different mindsets, strategies, and levels of involvement.

While business and investment are both integral to the world of finance and wealth creation, they are distinct in their methods, objectives, and roles. A business requires an active commitment of time, effort, and resources to develop and manage products, services, and operations, while investment is focused on growing wealth through financial strategies and market opportunities. By understanding the differences, you can better decide which path is right for you based on your own aspirations and resources.

Social Media: A Powerful Weapon, But...

In today's world, social media has become an undeniable force in shaping businesses. Start-ups like Sahyadri Farms, BioMee, The Farm, Fruitwala Bagayatdar, and Ganna Master have successfully leveraged this tool to build strong brands. Sahyadri, in particular, has emerged as a dominant player in agricultural exports, proving that farmer-led businesses can reach global markets when backed by the right strategy.

While many of us were busy debating politics, philosophy, and social issues online, these brands were silently building farmer networks and engaging with real customers. This difference in approach is why they have achieved long-term success, while many others continue chasing temporary social media validation.

It is common to see individuals and organizations exaggerating minor events just to garner likes and engagement. But at the same time, there are businesses that use social media to create meaningful connections with their target audience. Instead of merely broadcasting knowledge, they focus on learning and problem-solving, leading to a two-way interaction that fosters trust.

Such businesses use social media not just for promotion but as a tool to solve technical issues for their customers. As a result, their audience feels a sense of belonging, and the brand grows organically. In the case of agricultural businesses, farmers themselves have become brand ambassadors, promoting these businesses through social media.

A remarkable example of this is BioMee.

During the COVID-19 pandemic, Maharashtra's tomato farmers were struck by a fungal blight, leaving them devastated. The agriculture department struggled to provide clear solutions, while certain media outlets irresponsibly linked the issue to COVID-19, creating further confusion. Rumors spread that tomatoes could be a carrier of the virus, adding to the panic.

At a time when farmers were on the brink of financial ruin, BioMee stepped in. Instead of waiting for government intervention, they took their research labs directly to the fields, conducting on-ground experiments to find solutions. They launched an awareness campaign using news portals and social media, providing scientific explanations and practical remedies for farmers. Their transparency and problem-solving approach earned them trust, helping their business expand significantly.

This is a prime example of how social media can be used as a powerful weapon for positive change. However, like any weapon, it is a double-edged sword.

In India, social media, which was meant to be an information revolution, has also given rise to serious challenges. Misinformation spreads faster than ever, leading to historical distortions, political propaganda, and social unrest. Figures like Nehru and Gandhi, whose contributions to the country are well documented, are routinely ridiculed as part of an effort to rewrite narratives.

Fake news has elevated unworthy individuals into positions of power, while extremist groups—whether religious, political, or criminal—have exploited social media to amplify hate and violence. Infamous criminals like Lawrence Bishnoi, operating under the guise of Hindu extremism, and various Islamic and Hindutva fundamentalist groups are thriving in the digital space, spreading their ideology unchecked.

The real challenge is deciding what to consume and what to ignore.

For businesses, social media should be used strategically, not impulsively. Entrepreneurs must focus on building a responsible brand, attracting informed consumers, and staying away from divisive political agendas. The goal should not be to take left-wing or right-wing positions, but rather to create a space for positive engagement that leads to business growth and a progressive society.

In the end, the power of social media lies in how we choose to use it.

CHAPTER FOURTEEN

The Importance of Business Selection and Team Formation

Choosing the right business and assembling the right team are foundational to long- term success in the entrepreneurial world. The success of any business largely depends on the decisions made at the beginning—specifically, the choice of business model and the formation of a competent and diverse team. A one-person operation or a narrow-minded approach will often limit growth potential and opportunities, particularly in today's fast-paced, interconnected business environment.

The Role of Business Selection

When selecting a business, it's essential to choose something that not only aligns with your skills and interests but also fits well with market demand, customer needs, and future trends. Many entrepreneurs start businesses based on a passion or expertise they have, but overlooking the market landscape or consumer demands can result in wasted time and resources. Business selection is more than just picking a product or service; it's about understanding your target audience, assessing market trends, and making informed decisions that will position your business for growth.

The Importance of Team Formation

A business is never successful without the right team behind it. The team's skill set, diversity, and overall alignment with the company's vision and values can be the difference between success and failure. One common mistake entrepreneurs make is hiring people based on personal biases—such as selecting team members based on caste, religion, or family connections. While these factors may seem familiar or comfortable, they can limit the potential of your business.

In contrast, a diverse team brings different perspectives, skills, and ideas that can propel the business to new heights. A narrow mindset in team selection often results in a homogenous group that might struggle with innovation and decision-making. Diversity in experience, thought, and background can help bring in fresh ideas, challenge the status quo, and lead to better problem-solving.

The most successful businesses are those that recognize the value of open-mindedness and diversity when forming a team. Whether it's by selecting individuals from different industries, backgrounds, or even nationalities, bringing together a diverse set of strengths can lead to faster growth and more innovative solutions.

Understanding the Difference Between Product-Oriented and Customer-Oriented Business Models

When forming a business, it's also important to choose the right business model. The two primary types of business models are product-oriented and customer-oriented, each with its distinct focus and strategies. The model you choose will influence the direction of your company, your marketing efforts, and even the kind of team you need to build.

Product-Oriented Business Model

In a product-oriented business, the focus is on the development, manufacturing, and selling of products. Companies that follow this model are primarily concerned with producing high-quality products that meet certain standards or specifications, regardless of customer input. Their success is measured by how well the product performs in the market and the demand it generates.

Businesses like Apple, Nokia, Samsung, HP, Dell, and Swiggy are classic examples of product-oriented models. They either design their own products or sell third-party products, but their success is driven by the quality and uniqueness of their offerings. The product becomes the central factor driving sales, and much of the business's energy goes into innovation, research, and development to ensure their products stay relevant and desirable.

For businesses using this model, it's crucial to:

- Focus on creating innovative and high-quality products.
- Invest in research and development (R&D).
- Ensure product availability and reliable delivery.

Customer-Oriented Business Model

In contrast, a customer-oriented business focuses on understanding and fulfilling the needs of its customers. Rather than centring efforts on creating the best product, these businesses prioritize delivering the best customer experience by aligning their offerings with customer preferences, needs, and feedback.

Companies like Walmart, Amazon, Netflix, Big Bazaar, and Flipkart excel in this model. They often provide a range of products or services tailored to meet customer demands, rather than focusing on a single product. They understand that customer satisfaction and loyalty are key drivers of success, so their marketing and business strategies revolve around providing value to customers and continuously meeting their needs.

In this model, it's crucial to:

- Conduct regular market research to understand customer desires.
- Focus on providing excellent customer service.
- Ensure fast and efficient delivery or access to services.

Which Model to Choose?

Both business models can be highly successful, but choosing the right one depends on your product, industry, and vision for the company. For instance:

- If you have a unique product or invention that has the potential to change the market, a product-oriented model may be more suitable.

- If you're entering a highly competitive market with many similar products, focusing on customer needs and satisfaction through a customer-oriented model might be more effective.

In some cases, businesses may use a hybrid model, blending both approaches to create a comprehensive strategy that maximizes product appeal while also catering to customer satisfaction.

Ultimately, the selection of your business and the formation of your team are two of the most important decisions you'll make as an entrepreneur. By adopting an open-minded approach in both areas, you set the foundation for your company's success. Whether you follow a product-oriented or customer-oriented business model, having a clear vision, a diverse and capable team, and a deep understanding of your market will greatly increase your chances of building a sustainable and successful business.

Choosing a Business Based on Passion or Opportunity

When embarking on a new business venture, entrepreneurs often face a key decision: should they pursue a business based on their passions and personal interests, or should they seize an opportunity in the market, even if it doesn't align with their personal preferences? Both approaches have their merits, and choosing the right path depends on various factors, including market conditions, personal goals, and the type of business model you envision.

Passion-Based Business Ventures

Many entrepreneurs are driven by their passions, education, skills, and interests when selecting a business. This approach can be highly fulfilling because it allows individuals to work in areas they care deeply about. Passion fuels motivation and resilience, which are critical when facing the inevitable challenges of running a business.

However, it's important to understand that passion alone is not always enough to guarantee success. Just because you love a particular product or service doesn't necessarily mean that the market will respond the same way. Consumer preferences can be unpredictable, and aligning your business with your passion requires thorough market research to assess demand, competition, and sustainability.

Opportunity-Based Business Ventures

On the other hand, many entrepreneurs achieve success by identifying and seizing business opportunities, even if those opportunities do not align with their personal passions. This approach often involves recognizing gaps in the market, unmet needs, or emerging trends that offer potential for growth.

For example, I ventured into government tendering, focusing on a customer-oriented approach, which yielded success even though it wasn't directly tied to my personal interests. The opportunity was ripe, and by capitalizing on it, I was able to build a profitable business.

This type of opportunity-driven approach requires a mindset that is open to market demands and trends. It also demands a keen awareness of where there is potential for growth, even in areas outside of your personal passion. Entrepreneurs who focus on opportunities tend to be more pragmatic and flexible, willing to explore industries or ideas that may not initially excite them but hold significant promise.

Customer-Oriented vs. Product-Oriented Business Models

When starting any new venture, it's important to evaluate whether your business approach is customer-oriented or product-oriented. Both strategies have their own benefits and challenges:

- Customer-Oriented Business: In this model, the focus is on understanding customer needs and providing value. Businesses like Zomato and Swiggy exemplify this approach. By innovating in delivery services and focusing on customer convenience, they transformed the food service industry. Their success is largely due to their ability to identify and meet consumer demands.
- Product-Oriented Business: This approach focuses on creating and selling high-quality products, often with little regard for customer preferences. The key is innovation in the product itself. A strong product-focused approach can work if you have cutting-edge technology or a unique product that satisfies a niche market.

Whether your focus is on customer or product will depend on the nature of your business. Both models can lead to success, but your strategy should be tailored to the market you're entering and the resources at your disposal.

Understanding Brand Creator Darshanbhai Patel

To illustrate the power of brand creation, consider the example of Darshanbhai Patel, the visionary behind renowned brands like Fog, Move, Crack, Ichguard, Dermikul, and Decold. His name is synonymous with entrepreneurship and brand-building in India. Patel's journey serves as an excellent example of how strategic thinking, clear planning, and consistent innovation can result in the creation of successful brands that become household names.

Darshanbhai Patel didn't just create these brands for the sake of branding; he ensured that they represented high quality and reliability. His success story is not merely about coming up with catchy names for products; it's about understanding the market, investing in top- notch production, and building a strong distribution network.

His brands, after reaching a dominant position in the market, were eventually sold to Reckitt Benckiser, a global consumer goods company, for billions of rupees. This sale was not only a reflection of the quality of his products but also a result of his strategic thinking in positioning the brands within the market.

Despite his success, Darshanbhai does not indulge in motivational speaking or public forums. His work and achievements serve as the best motivation for aspiring entrepreneurs.

His story highlights the importance of focusing on meaningful work rather than seeking external validation or inspiration from motivational speakers. By focusing on practical, impactful business strategies, entrepreneurs can achieve success that speaks for itself.

Key Takeaways

- Passion can drive you to start a business, but opportunity often holds more practical promise.
- Both customer-oriented and product-oriented models have their strengths, and understanding which suits your business idea is crucial.

- Entrepreneurs like Darshanbhai Patel prove that success comes from creating value through high-quality products and strategic market positioning—not just from having a great brand name.
- Focus on meaningful work and innovation, rather than relying solely on external sources of motivation. Success in business is often about consistent effort, strategic thinking, and the willingness to learn from the market.

The Importance of Team Selection and Building

When it comes to business success, it's crucial to remember that no business thrives on the efforts of just one person. A successful business is built on the collaboration and synergy of a capable team, and choosing the right team members is key to sustained growth and success. The team should be formed with individuals who value responsibility, duty, and shared vision rather than focusing on positions, prestige, or personal gain. This principle not only applies to business but can also be seen in other areas, such as politics, where unity and purpose can lead to significant outcomes.

The Politics of Team Selection: A Historical Perspective

To understand the importance of open-minded and responsible team-building, we can look back at the Indian freedom struggle. During this period, leaders from various backgrounds, with different ideologies, came together to form the Indian National Congress. They set aside their differences to work toward a common goal—India's independence. This united and purpose-driven approach ultimately led to success.

However, in the years following independence, politics became more about position, power, and prestige, leading to inefficiencies and stagnation in the political system. The focus shifted away from responsibility and duty, which led to corruption and political decay. This historical shift serves as a powerful lesson: poor team selection and a focus on shallow goals can result in long-term negative impacts, not just in business but also in societal structures.

Building a Business Team with Responsibility and Vision

Returning to the topic of team-building for business, it's important to emphasize that for a business to thrive, the team should be skilled, responsible, and aligned with the long- term vision of the organization. Here's what to focus on when selecting your business team:

1. Skills and Expertise: Team members must have technical knowledge of the product or services you offer. However, the emphasis should be on having a well-rounded team that also possesses qualities like honesty and willingness to take responsibility. Without these core values, even the most skilled team can falter.

2. Unity and Responsibility: For a team to function well, there must be a sense of unity and shared responsibility. While team members don't need to share every personal experience, it's crucial that no one in the team undermines or sabotages others. A team should function like a family, where mutual respect and collective growth are prioritized over individual glory.

3. Experience and Balance: While it's important to have passionate and enthusiastic individuals, it's equally crucial to have experienced individuals on the team. These experienced members bring valuable insights, especially in terms of how leadership mistakes can affect the business. However, experience alone is not enough. If the experienced individuals have a narrow mindset or a negative attitude, they can be detrimental to the team. It's important to strike a balance between enthusiasm and experience.

4. Camaraderie Over Hierarchy: In a successful team, the hierarchical structure should be as flat as possible. Even if you're the owner of the business, it's important to avoid adopting a boss-like attitude. A bossy attitude can create unnecessary barriers between you and your team, hindering communication and collaboration. Instead, fostering a spirit of camaraderie and teamwork will drive the business forward. In my own experience, I've had to let go of individuals who had a "boss" attitude in favour of those who embraced a more collaborative mindset. This decision, though difficult in the short term, has proven to be beneficial for the long-term health of the business.

Real-World Example: A Mentorship Story

One of my valued colleagues, Mahadev Gawli, who I met through Facebook, exemplifies the qualities that make a strong team member. He understands the importance of respecting everyone's role in the team, regardless of their position. For instance, when he introduces a team member, he refers to them simply as "my colleague" instead of using hierarchical terms like "my manager" or "my worker." This simple act of equality and respect fosters a culture where everyone feels valued, and no one's contribution is diminished.

Another key mentor of mine, Kishore Raktate, has an insightful perspective when dealing with people who focus on criticizing others rather than adding value. He often says, "In the pursuit of finding others' faults, you will miss the opportunity to expand your own work." This perspective is especially relevant today, when many people engage in online criticism but don't contribute positively themselves. Such individuals, with a negative or self- centred mindset, have no place in your core business or team.

Key Principles for Effective Team Building

1. Collaborative Spirit: Focus on creating a team that values mutual respect and shared goals. Everyone in the team should understand the broader vision and work toward it together.
2. Balanced Skill Set: While skills and expertise are important, a team should also prioritize qualities like honesty, responsibility, and humility.
3. Avoid Negative Influences: Keep a watchful eye for individuals who bring a toxic or narrow mindset into the team. These individuals can often disrupt the team dynamic and harm the overall success of the business.
4. Empowerment Over Hierarchy: Foster a culture of respect where the hierarchy doesn't become a barrier to communication. Every member should feel valued, regardless of their position in the company.

The success of any business hinges on the strength of its team. Choosing the right people, fostering a collaborative environment, and ensuring alignment with the business's long-term goals is essential for sustainable growth. Focus on values like honesty, responsibility, and mutual respect while steering clear of individuals who disrupt the team's unity or focus solely on personal gain. As the adage goes, "A team is only as strong as its weakest link," so ensure that every member is a valuable contributor to the collective success of the business.

Important Aspects of Building a Strong Business Team

Building a successful business isn't just about having the right product or service—it's about having the right team. A strong team can make all the difference, and key to that is fostering effective communication, adaptability, and ethics. When these elements are in place, the team can handle challenges, stay motivated, and grow in alignment with the business's goals.

The Role of Communication in Team Success

Effective communication is at the heart of any strong team. Without clear communication, misunderstandings can arise, tasks can be delayed, and the team's motivation can dwindle. Communication allows teams to stay on the same page, share feedback, and implement plans efficiently. Moreover, when communication is transparent, it helps to reduce errors and clarify the path forward.

An open and clear communication culture also encourages learning from mistakes. Teams that can acknowledge errors and discuss them constructively are better equipped to adapt to challenges. With continuous learning, team members can stay relevant, meet market demands, and enhance their skillsets.

Adapting to Change and Embracing Technology

In today's fast-paced world, businesses must be adaptable to survive and thrive. The most successful teams are those that embrace new technologies and continuously seek ways to innovate. This flexibility allows businesses to stay competitive by responding to market changes and leveraging new tools to improve efficiency.

A business team must also be willing to learn and grow as conditions evolve. Whether it's adopting new software, refining processes, or adjusting business models, a growth mindset is crucial. Teams that are open to change and focused on development are more likely to overcome challenges and succeed in the long run.

Leading by Example: Integrity and Ethics

A strong business team starts with strong leadership. The founder or business leader must lead by example, setting a high standard of integrity. The famous quote from *Game of Thrones*—"If you want to give orders, first learn how to follow them"—reminds us that leadership isn't about commanding from above but about modelling the behaviour you want to see in your team.

This is reinforced by a quote from Prof. Dr. Mahebub Syed: "If you want others to trust your words, you must first honour your own words." In business, like in life, ethical behaviour builds trust. Adhering to principles of honesty and integrity—even when it's tempting to take shortcuts—establishes a foundation of trust within the team. Leaders who do so create a team that reflects these same values. Trust and integrity, in turn, make it easier to navigate the inevitable challenges that come with growing a business.

The Reality of Struggle and Adaptation

It's often said that marriage or the defeat of a villain marks the end of struggle and the beginning of happiness. But in business and life, the reality is different. Struggle is a constant companion, and business success isn't about avoiding difficulties but about learning to navigate them. As entrepreneurs, we face challenges at every step, from team-building to market competition to managing growth. Struggle is inherent, and accepting that makes the process of building a business much more manageable.

In both family life and entrepreneurship, adjustment is key. As we evolve in business, we must recognize that strict adherence to rules isn't always feasible. The ability to adapt is crucial, but it's important not to disregard rules entirely. Balancing structure and flexibility helps businesses grow while maintaining quality and staying aligned with core values.

Maintaining Quality During Growth

As businesses expand, the temptation to compromise on quality can arise. Scaling often comes with the risk of losing the essence of what made the business successful in the first place. To maintain quality while expanding, businesses need to establish clear strategies that align both the team and the organization with the company's core mission. This ensures that growth doesn't dilute the company's value or the trust it has built with its customers.

A competent and trustworthy team is essential for this. A team that is committed to the business's vision will help the business grow sustainably without losing its positive momentum or compromising quality.

Business success is a dynamic balance of several key factors: communication, adaptability, ethics, and continuous self-improvement. When these principles are in place, entrepreneurs can build strong, reliable teams that are capable of achieving long-term success. By leading with integrity, embracing change, and fostering a culture of trust, business owners can create teams that drive progress and help the business thrive in an ever-changing world.

CHAPTER FIFTEEN

Fearlessness Combined with Risk Management for Success

In the realms of entrepreneurship and business, fearlessness stands out as a cornerstone trait for success. When paired with effective risk management, this attitude becomes a powerful force that drives decision-making and enables individuals and teams to confront challenges with courage and precision. Every business opportunity comes with its own set of uncertainties, and it is the fearless entrepreneur who transforms these uncertainties into stepping stones for growth.

The Power of Fearlessness in Business

Fearlessness is not the absence of fear, but rather the ability to act despite it. Like a candle that illuminates a dark room, fearlessness enables entrepreneurs to dispel the darkness of doubt and hesitation. It is a mindset that fosters confidence and empowers business leaders to tackle obstacles head-on, without regret or hesitation. While challenges may be unavoidable, how one responds to them determines the outcome. Fearlessness, therefore, becomes a critical tool for maintaining clarity and focus during turbulent times.

Consider the popular slogan "Fear is the enemy, but victory lies beyond it," often used by brands like Mountain Dew. It captures the essence of entrepreneurship: success lies on the other side of fear. History provides us with numerous examples of individuals who achieved greatness by overcoming fear. One such story is that of Rajmata Jijau and Shivaji Maharaj, who, during a time dominated by the oppressive Mughal rule under Aurangzeb, built the foundation of the Maratha Empire. Their fearless approach and commitment to establishing a just and free kingdom—swarajya—have left an indelible mark on history.

Their courage teaches us that fearlessness isn't just about defeating enemies or challenges; it's about creating something meaningful and lasting. Similarly, in the business world, the goal isn't just to dominate markets but to serve customers with a fearless and service-oriented mindset. This approach fosters trust, loyalty, and long-term growth.

Fearlessness and Risk Management

Fearlessness does not mean recklessness. While being bold is crucial, every decision in business must be backed by calculated risks. Entrepreneurs who act without considering potential outcomes can jeopardize their ventures. On the other hand, those who assess risks thoughtfully while maintaining a fearless attitude can seize opportunities others may overlook.

Risk management involves understanding, analysing, and mitigating uncertainties while maintaining the courage to act. It is this combination that separates successful businesses from stagnant ones. A fearless entrepreneur knows when to act decisively, even when the path ahead is unclear. Hesitation caused by fear can lead to missed opportunities, while calculated action can pave the way for success.

The Role of Mistakes in Success

Mistakes are an inevitable part of any entrepreneurial journey. However, a fear of mistakes can stifle creativity, innovation, and progress. Fearlessness allows entrepreneurs to embrace mistakes as opportunities for learning and growth. Each error provides valuable lessons that refine decision-making and improve future strategies.

Successful entrepreneurs view mistakes as stepping stones rather than roadblocks. They adapt, learn, and evolve, using their experiences to strengthen their businesses. This mindset fosters resilience, builds confidence, and cultivates a culture of innovation within their teams.

Building a Fearless Team

Just as Shivaji Maharaj relied on a core group of trusted warriors who shared his vision, businesses need managers and workers who embody fearlessness and a shared commitment to success. A fearless team is one that is:

1. Service-Oriented: Focused on improving customer experiences and addressing customer needs with agility and creativity.
2. Collaborative: United by a shared vision and mutual trust, ensuring every team member contributes meaningfully.
3. Adaptable: Open to embracing change, experimenting with new ideas, and leveraging technology for growth.
4. Resilient: Equipped to handle failures and setbacks with a mindset of continuous improvement.

Leadership plays a crucial role in cultivating fearlessness within a team. By setting an example of bold decision-making, ethical behaviour, and adaptability, leaders can inspire their teams to adopt a fearless approach.

Fearlessness in Decision-Making

In a highly competitive business landscape, hesitation can be costly. Bold and fearless decision-making, especially when supported by thorough risk analysis, enables businesses to stay ahead of competitors. It is this ability to act swiftly and strategically that sets successful entrepreneurs apart. By balancing fearlessness with a practical understanding of risks, businesses can innovate, adapt, and grow in dynamic markets.

Fearlessness, when combined with effective risk management, is a critical ingredient for entrepreneurial success. It empowers leaders and teams to face challenges head-on, embrace mistakes as learning opportunities, and make bold, strategic decisions. Cultivating fearlessness within an organization builds confidence, resilience, and a foundation for sustainable growth. Ultimately, the fearless entrepreneur is one who sees beyond fear to seize opportunities and create a legacy of success.

Embracing Change and Fearlessness in the Face of Technological Advances

The business world is in a constant state of evolution, driven by emerging technologies, shifting trends, and new challenges. Change, as the saying goes, is the only constant. To thrive in such an environment, it is essential to embrace change fearlessly. This mindset enables businesses to adapt, innovate, and grow, even in the face of uncertainty.

The Early Fear of Technology

History is rich with examples of initial resistance to technological advances. When computers first entered the market, they were met with widespread scepticism and fear. Many believed these machines would replace human jobs, leading to opposition from various political and social groups, including thinkers from both left and right ideologies. However, over time, these very groups came to accept and even depend on information technology.

This shift underscores a universal truth: fear of change often stems from a lack of understanding. Once the potential benefits of technology became clear, even its staunchest critics embraced it. The digital revolution reshaped industries, societies, and political landscapes, demonstrating that those who adopt and adapt to new technologies early are the ones who ultimately succeed.

The Success Stories of Fearless Adaptation

Some of India's most prominent IT companies, like TCS, Infosys, and Wipro, are prime examples of businesses that embraced technological change without hesitation. During a time when the introduction of computers was viewed with suspicion, these companies recognized the transformative potential of technology. Instead of succumbing to fear, they confronted change head-on, pioneering solutions that not only revolutionized their operations but also elevated India's position in the global IT sector.

Their fearless acceptance of change didn't just benefit their businesses—it created a ripple effect, fostering a culture of innovation and positioning India as a leader in the technology industry. This success would not have been possible without the willingness to take risks and the vision to see beyond immediate fears.

Fearlessness Inspires Confidence in Teams

The attitude of a leader or organization towards change directly influences the team. Fearlessness in the face of new challenges fosters a culture of confidence, resilience, and openness within the team. When leaders approach technological advancements with curiosity and determination, it sets an example that inspires others to adopt the same mindset.

This ripple effect empowers teams to:

- Be Open to New Ideas: A fearless approach encourages team members to experiment and innovate without fear of failure.
- Adapt to Challenges: Teams become more resilient, capable of navigating uncertainties and crises effectively.
- Stay Competitive: By embracing change, businesses ensure they remain relevant and ahead of competitors in a rapidly evolving market.

Learning Through Risks and Mistakes

The road to success is rarely without missteps. However, businesses that fearlessly take risks and learn from their mistakes are better positioned to grow. Each failure becomes a stepping stone to greater understanding and improved decision-making.

Incorporating new technologies often involves trial and error, but the willingness to embrace these trials leads to breakthroughs. Whether it's automating processes, adopting artificial intelligence, or leveraging data analytics, fearlessness in experimentation paves the way for long-term success.

The Competitive Edge of Embracing Change

In today's fast-paced market, hesitation can be costly. Businesses that fail to adapt to technological advances risk falling behind. On the other hand, organizations that actively seek out and integrate new technologies gain a competitive edge. They streamline operations, enhance customer experiences, and innovate in ways that set them apart.

Fearlessness in embracing change not only drives growth but also builds resilience, enabling businesses to weather economic downturns, technological disruptions, and shifting consumer demands.

The journey of technology and its integration into business serves as a powerful reminder that fear of change is natural but must be overcome to achieve success. Fearlessness, combined with an open-minded approach, empowers businesses to:

- Adapt to technological advances with confidence.
- Foster a culture of innovation and resilience within their teams.
- Build long-term competitive advantages in a dynamic marketplace.

By embracing change fearlessly, businesses not only navigate the present but also position themselves for a prosperous future. Fearlessness is not merely a mindset; it is the foundation of progress in an ever-evolving world.

The Importance of Risk Management in Business

A fearless mindset is a valuable trait for entrepreneurs, as it fuels bold decision-making and the ability to face challenges head-on. However, fearlessness alone is not enough to guarantee success. Without a well-structured approach to managing risks, even the bravest ventures can falter. The interplay between fearlessness and effective risk management forms the cornerstone of sustainable success in any business.

Why Fearlessness Alone is Insufficient

Courage is often celebrated in business, but it must be paired with wisdom and caution. A fearless attitude that ignores risks can lead to impulsive decisions with devastating consequences. To illustrate, consider this analogy: if someone fearlessly walks into a pride of hungry lions, the outcome is obvious—and it's not in their favour. Similarly, in business, boldness without a clear understanding of the associated risks can lead to failure.

Risk management serves as the bridge between ambition and achievement. It allows businesses to navigate uncertainties by identifying, analysing, and addressing potential pitfalls. This process enables entrepreneurs to pursue opportunities with confidence, knowing they are prepared for the challenges ahead.

Understanding Risk Management

Risk management involves identifying potential threats, assessing their impact, and formulating strategies to mitigate them. It's not just about avoiding risks but also about recognizing opportunities that may arise from them. Effective risk management requires:

1. Identification of Risks: Understanding what could go wrong in various aspects of the business, such as finances, operations, competition, or market trends.
2. Assessment of Impact: Evaluating the severity and likelihood of risks to prioritize them effectively.
3. Strategic Planning: Creating contingency plans to address potential risks and minimize their impact on the business.
4. Monitoring and Adapting: Continuously tracking risks and adjusting strategies as circumstances change.

Learning from Experience: A Real-Life Example

In 2010, during the growth phase of Chavdi, I experienced firsthand the consequences of inadequate risk management. While expanding into 8-10 districts, our ambition outpaced our preparation. We aimed to build a larger brand without fully understanding the challenges or ensuring we had the necessary resources and strategies in place. Internal conflicts arose, and ultimately, the company couldn't sustain itself.

Contrast this with the success story of Sahyadri Agrovet, founded by Nitin Hase, an agricultural graduate from Sangamner. Starting small, they focused on a specific niche—selling machines like kadhba kutti (cashew processing machines). Gradually, they expanded into dairy products and became a significant name in the industry. Their approach highlights several key lessons:

- Gradual Expansion: They built their business step by step, consolidating their position before taking on bigger challenges.
- Market Understanding: They identified genuine market needs and tailored their offerings accordingly.

- Effective Risk Management: By assessing and addressing risks at each stage, they created a solid foundation for growth.

This comparison demonstrates that while ambition is essential, it must be grounded in a realistic understanding of risks and a clear strategy for managing them.

Common Pitfalls in Risk Management

Many entrepreneurs fail to adequately manage risks due to the following reasons:

1. Overconfidence: Assuming that ambition alone is enough to overcome challenges.
2. Insufficient Planning: Diving into ventures without a thorough understanding of market dynamics or operational requirements.
3. Neglecting Small Wins: Overlooking the importance of starting small and building momentum gradually.
4. Lack of Monitoring: Failing to revisit and revise strategies in response to changing circumstances.

The Role of Calculated Risk-Taking

Risk management doesn't mean avoiding risks entirely; it means taking calculated risks.
This involves:

- Weighing potential rewards against potential losses.
- Ensuring the business has the capacity to absorb setbacks.
- Preparing contingency plans to address unexpected outcomes.

By adopting this approach, businesses can seize opportunities while minimizing the likelihood of adverse effects.

Key Takeaways for Entrepreneurs

- Evaluate Risks Thoroughly: Understand the potential impact of each risk and plan accordingly.
- Balance Ambition with Practicality: Dream big but ensure your foundation is strong and your strategies are realistic.
- Learn from Mistakes: View failures as opportunities for growth and refinement.
- Adapt and Evolve: Stay vigilant and be prepared to adjust your plans as new risks and opportunities emerge.

Risk management is an indispensable component of business success. While fearlessness propels entrepreneurs to take bold steps, effective risk management ensures these steps are taken wisely. By balancing ambition with careful planning and preparation, businesses can navigate challenges, seize opportunities, and achieve sustainable growth.

The Need for a Reality Check Advisor in Business

Success can often lead to complacency. Once entrepreneurs experience some level of achievement, it's not uncommon for them to feel as though they've mastered their domain. However, this mindset can be perilous. As the seasoned entrepreneur D.R. Patil once said, *"The day you think you know everything, that will be the day of your downfall."* This wisdom serves as a powerful reminder that humility and a willingness to learn are essential traits for sustained growth in both business and life.

Why a Reality Check is Crucial

Arrogance and overconfidence can isolate a businessperson from valuable advice and constructive criticism. Surrounding oneself with "yes-men"—people who agree with every decision without question—can be detrimental, as it fosters an echo chamber that blinds one to reality. Without a reality check, decisions are made based on assumptions rather than facts, leading to mistakes that could otherwise have been avoided.

Even leaders at the pinnacle of success, such as Prime Ministers and CEOs, rely on advisors who offer candid feedback. Historical examples like India's first Prime Minister, Jawaharlal Nehru, demonstrate the power of having a diverse and expert advisory team. His cabinet, composed of thought leaders from various fields, helped lay the foundations of modern

India. Similarly, great leaders like Atal Bihari Vajpayee, Dr. Manmohan Singh, and Sharad Pawar surrounded themselves with knowledgeable advisors who provided guidance across a broad spectrum of issues.

In the business world, this principle holds just as true. Successful entrepreneurs often attribute their achievements to the guidance of mentors and advisors who helped them navigate complex challenges and seize opportunities.

The Role of a Reality Check Advisor

A *reality check advisor* serves several critical functions in a business:

1. Providing Honest Feedback: They don't shy away from challenging your ideas or pointing out flaws in your plans.
2. Offering Diverse Perspectives: Their expertise in various fields broadens your understanding of potential challenges and solutions.
3. Balancing Optimism with Realism: While optimism is essential for driving ambition, advisors help ground your plans in practicality.
4. Encouraging Lifelong Learning: They emphasize the importance of continuous growth and staying informed about trends and developments.
5. Mitigating Risks: By highlighting blind spots, advisors help prevent costly mistakes and guide strategic decision-making.

Lessons from Personal Experience

During my own entrepreneurial journey, I've faced moments where I, too, was tempted to adopt an air of expertise. But each time, I was reminded of the importance of staying grounded by mentors like D.R. Patil. His advice to focus on action rather than boasting has been a guiding principle for me. Through exposure to various experiences—government schemes, political campaigns, and interactions with professionals—I've learned the value of listening and learning from those around me.

I've also seen the consequences of neglecting this principle. In one instance, my team and I pursued ambitious expansion plans without adequately seeking external advice. The result was a business collapse due to internal conflicts and poor decision-making. On the other hand, businesses that prioritized strategic advice and maintained open communication with advisors thrived in the same competitive landscape.

Distinguishing Shallow Inspiration from Deep Insights

Motivational speakers often inspire us to dream big, but their knowledge can sometimes lack depth. In contrast, advisors with real-world experience, like authors Devdutt Pattanaik and entrepreneurs like Vikas Divyakirti, provide practical insights rooted in reality. Their advice encourages a positive mindset while emphasizing critical thinking and evidence-based decision-making.

The Power of Advisory Teams

Advisors are indispensable, especially as businesses grow and face increasingly complex challenges. Whether it's selecting the right technology, crafting a marketing strategy, or managing finances, advisors bring specialized knowledge and experience that can make a significant difference.

Leaders like Prime Minister Narendra Modi demonstrate how surrounding oneself with experts ensures informed decision-making. His reliance on a diverse team of advisors has enabled him to craft impactful policies and navigate global challenges effectively. The same principle applies to businesses: having advisors who challenge your assumptions, offer constructive criticism, and encourage innovative thinking is key to long-term success.

How to Cultivate a Strong Advisory Network To build a robust network of advisors:

1. Seek Diversity: Look for individuals with expertise in different areas—finance, technology, marketing, and operations.
2. Encourage Open Dialogue: Create an environment where advisors feel comfortable sharing honest feedback.
3. Learn Continuously: Attend seminars, exhibitions, and workshops to stay updated and gain fresh perspectives.

4. Evaluate Regularly: Assess the effectiveness of your advisors and be open to adding new voices to your team.

A *reality check advisor* is more than just a mentor; they are a cornerstone of thoughtful decision-making and sustainable success. Their role in providing honest, constructive feedback and diverse perspectives cannot be overstated. Whether in politics, business, or personal life, surrounding yourself with trusted advisors who challenge you to think critically will keep you grounded, informed, and prepared to tackle the challenges of an ever-changing world.

Increasing Decision-Making Ability Through Experience

Decision-making is an art and a skill that develops over time, shaped by our experiences and the challenges we face. While books, seminars, and advisors provide valuable insights, they cannot replace the personal growth that comes from enduring and overcoming obstacles firsthand.

Many people believe that reading a certain book or listening to a specific speaker will unlock the secret to success. But the reality is far from it. Success is not the result of merely acquiring theoretical knowledge; it comes from integrating that knowledge through practical application. No book, no matter how profound, can teach you the lessons that life's challenges provide.

Experience: The Real Teacher

You may have noticed individuals who seem unqualified but manage to achieve great success, whether in politics, business, or other fields. In politics, for instance, it's not uncommon for seemingly average or even questionable candidates to win elections, while highly capable, thoughtful individuals are overlooked. This happens because success often hinges on understanding and addressing the immediate needs of people, rather than on intellectual prowess or vision. Similarly, in business, those who take risks and seize opportunities tend to fare better than those who wait for perfect conditions.

This underscores an important truth: success is not about shortcuts or formulas—it's about persistence, adaptability, and learning from every experience.

The Long-Term View

In decision-making, the results of our actions may not always be immediately visible. Decisions that seem to fail in the short term might set the stage for success a decade later. Conversely, what appears as instant success may crumble over time. Therefore, the focus should not be solely on immediate outcomes but on the long-term growth and learning that comes from the process.

Striving to make completely safe decisions that guarantee no harm to anyone is an impossible standard. If we try to avoid all risks, we may end up doing nothing at all. It's essential to find a balance: make decisions that align with your values, minimize harm, and accept that no choice is ever entirely risk-free.

Learning from Great Thinkers

The process of improving decision-making is enriched by learning from the wisdom of great thinkers and spiritual leaders. Figures like Osho Rajneesh, BK Shivani, Acharya Prashant, and Vikas Divyakirti, as well as the teachings of Lord Gautama Buddha, Lord Mahavir, the Bhagavad Gita, and the Vedas, offer profound lessons. These teachings encourage reflection, mindfulness, and the cultivation of a flexible mindset that accepts change and uncertainty.

Even seemingly simple stories, such as the Jataka tales or Arabian Nights, carry deep insights about human behaviour, the nature of challenges, and the art of navigating life's complexities. Engaging with such wisdom expands our perspective and helps us approach decisions with clarity and confidence.

The Humility of True Knowledge

One of the most important lessons in decision-making is recognizing the limits of our knowledge. Even the greatest minds in science and philosophy, from Newton to Einstein, never claimed to have complete understanding of the universe. Similarly, in business, no one can claim to have all the answers. Sharad Joshi, a renowned farmer leader, exemplified this humility when he told his colleagues, *"I don't have answers to all the questions, but let's come together and try to find them."*

This mindset—of collaboration, exploration, and openness—fosters growth and innovation. It reminds us that the journey of learning is continuous and that every experience, whether successful or not, contributes to our understanding.

Practical Steps to Enhance Decision-Making

1. Start Small, Learn Big: Begin by making smaller decisions and observing their outcomes. Use each experience as a learning opportunity to refine your approach.
2. Reflect Regularly: After every decision, take time to evaluate what went well, what didn't, and why. This reflection strengthens your ability to adapt in future scenarios.
3. Embrace Uncertainty: Understand that uncertainty is inherent in every decision. The goal is not to eliminate risk but to manage it effectively.
4. Seek Diverse Perspectives: Listen to advisors, read widely, and engage with people from different fields. Diverse input often leads to better-informed decisions.
5. Stay Humble: Acknowledge that you will never have all the answers. Focus on learning and growing, rather than striving for perfection.
6. Take Action: Overthinking can lead to paralysis. Accept that some level of risk is inevitable and take decisive steps toward your goals.

Decision-making ability grows not through passive consumption of knowledge but through active engagement with life's challenges. Books, advisors, and seminars are valuable tools, but they are only starting points. The true development of this skill lies in your willingness to take risks, make mistakes, and learn from them.

As you navigate the complexities of life and business, remember that no one has the ultimate truth. The journey of growth is a continuous process, shaped by experience, reflection, and an open mind. By combining wisdom from external sources with your own lived experiences, you will steadily increase your ability to make thoughtful, impactful decisions.

The Importance of Advisors and Making Informed Decisions

The role of advisors in any journey—whether personal, professional, or entrepreneurial—is invaluable. They provide insights, guidance, and a fresh perspective based on their own experiences. These individuals often act as mentors, helping us navigate challenges and recognize opportunities that we might overlook on our own. While advisors don't possess the magical formula for success, their wisdom can illuminate paths we may not have considered.

Why Advisors Are Essential

Advisors are not just guides; they are partners in decision-making. Their importance lies in the following areas:

1. Broadening Perspectives: Advisors bring diverse viewpoints, enabling us to look at problems from angles we might have missed.
2. Learning from Their Mistakes: By understanding the mistakes they've made, we can avoid similar pitfalls.
3. Mitigating Risks: They help us identify and evaluate risks, ensuring that decisions are well-informed and calculated.
4. Confidence Boosters: A good advisor doesn't just solve problems; they inspire confidence in our ability to make the right choices.
5. Support During Tough Times: Whether facing financial, emotional, or strategic dilemmas, advisors act as a stabilizing force, offering both solutions and encouragement.

The Art of Choosing Advisors

The effectiveness of an advisor depends heavily on their mindset and approach. Surrounding yourself with the wrong kind of advisors can lead to poor outcomes, regardless of their expertise.

- Open-Mindedness: Advisors who are willing to explore new ideas and think creatively are invaluable.
- Constructive Criticism: Choose someone who is honest and direct, offering critical feedback rather than just affirmations.
- Alignment with Goals: Advisors should understand your vision and align their guidance with your objectives.

- Diverse Skill Sets: A mix of advisors with expertise in various areas—finance, strategy, marketing, and technology—ensures comprehensive guidance.

Lessons from Fiction: Advisors in Game of Thrones

Fiction often mirrors reality, and HBO's *Game of Thrones* offers excellent lessons about the value of good advisors.

- Tyrion Lannister: Despite his personal flaws, Tyrion evolves into a wise political advisor. His ability to learn from his mistakes and guide others, like Jon Snow, demonstrates the transformative power of good counsel.
- Cersei Lannister: Cersei's downfall serves as a cautionary tale about arrogance and ignoring good advice. Even with immense power and resources, her refusal to listen leads to her undoing.
- Daenerys Targaryen: Daenerys's journey highlights the importance of self-awareness and understanding limits. Though she achieves great victories, her failure to heed advice and recognize when to pause ultimately leads to her tragic end.

These characters exemplify the consequences of listening—or failing to listen—to advisors, reflecting real-life scenarios in business, politics, and beyond.

The Reality of Ignored Advice

In real life, as in fiction, ignoring good advice often results in unnecessary challenges. Whether in business or politics, we've all seen individuals whose success is hindered by their inability to accept guidance. This underscores the importance of humility and the willingness to learn.

- Listening Actively: True listening involves more than hearing; it requires understanding and processing the insights offered.
- Extracting Value: Not every piece of advice will be applicable. The key is to discern the valuable aspects and integrate them into your decisions.

- Balancing Input and Instinct: While advice is crucial, your final decision should be a blend of external insights and your intuition.

Gaining Experience to Make Informed Decisions

Ultimately, even the best advice is only as good as the experience and understanding of the person receiving it. Experience sharpens our ability to evaluate advice and make sound decisions.

1. Practical Application: Use advice as a guide, but test its validity in real-world scenarios.
2. Reflect on Outcomes: Evaluate the results of your decisions to learn what worked and what didn't.
3. Continuous Learning: Stay open to new knowledge and insights, even as you grow more experienced.

Advisors play a critical role in helping us make informed decisions, but their guidance is only effective when paired with our own growth and experience. By choosing the right advisors and maintaining an open mind, we can navigate challenges more effectively and achieve greater success.

Remember, the ultimate responsibility for any decision lies with us. The battle is ours to fight, and the consequences—whether success or failure—are ours to bear. With the right guidance, however, we can tip the scales in our favour and make decisions that lead to long- term growth and fulfillment.

Guidance from the Thoughts and Actions of Shivaji Maharaj

The concept of Swarajya introduced by Chatrapati Shivaji Maharaj remains an enduring source of inspiration. Across India and beyond, his governance and leadership continue to be studied and analyzed, not just as a historical empire, but as a visionary model of effective management and leadership. His journey was not just about conquering land—it was about building a people-centric administration, grounded in strategy, organization, and a deep sense of responsibility toward his subjects. Even in today's world, the principles he followed offer valuable lessons for individuals, entrepreneurs, and leaders alike.

The idea of Swarajya was first envisioned by Rajmata Jijabai and Shahaji Raje, but it was Shivaji Maharaj who turned it into a reality. His time was filled with kings who fought wars for personal gain, yet the Bhosale dynasty focused on creating a just and independent state. This required carefully training soldiers from farming communities, fostering strong leadership, and implementing well-structured governance policies. His Asthapradhan Mandal (Council of Eight Ministers) played a key role in translating vision into action.

When Shivaji Maharaj first laid out the concept of Swarajya, many must have dismissed it as a mere dream. But he had a clear goal, which he shared with his commanders and people, making them active participants in his mission. His leadership style ensured that his entire administration and army were aligned with a single purpose. He made effective use of available resources, identified opportunities even in adversity, and built a resilient and self-sufficient system.

This approach mirrors what modern entrepreneurs must do. Any startup, business, or enterprise requires the same principles—strategic planning, resource optimization, team-building, and disciplined execution. Just as Swarajya wasn't built in a day, businesses don't become successful overnight. Every idea needs a solid plan, supported by hard work, courage, and adaptability.

Shivaji Maharaj had the ability to take the right decisions at the right time. He not only listened to his trusted intelligence chief Bahirji Naik but also valued the inputs of common soldiers and villagers. His flexibility in adjusting strategies based on ground realities was a key factor in his success. Similarly, businesses must study market trends, adopt new strategies, and remain open to transformation.

One of Shivaji Maharaj's greatest skills was team-building. He handpicked loyal and skilled warriors, trained them rigorously, and delegated leadership roles to the most capable individuals. In business, too, no entrepreneur can succeed alone. Identifying the right people, empowering them with responsibility, and trusting them to execute plans is essential for long-term success. A strong organization thrives on distributed leadership, just as Shivaji Maharaj's empire did.

His political intelligence was just as remarkable as his military prowess. While he fought battles fearlessly, he also engaged in diplomacy when required. He carefully navigated his relationships with the Mughal Empire, Adilshahi, and the British, choosing when to fight and when to negotiate.

Business leaders, too, must balance aggression with wisdom, understanding that success is not always about direct confrontation but about choosing battles wisely.

Just as Swarajya faced numerous challenges, every business will inevitably encounter competition, financial struggles, market fluctuations, and unforeseen crises. Shivaji Maharaj's core policy was "Identify opportunities and avoid unnecessary risks." This principle remains relevant in business as well—entrepreneurs must be vigilant, adaptive, and capable of turning challenges into opportunities.

His deep sense of social responsibility also set him apart. Unlike other rulers, who focused solely on expansion, Shivaji Maharaj worked for the welfare of his people, ensuring fair governance, economic stability, and strong agricultural policies. This philosophy is why businesses like the Tata Group and Jain Irrigation from Jalgaon stand out—they prioritize public welfare alongside profit. Companies that serve a greater purpose earn lasting respect and loyalty.

Above all, Shivaji Maharaj's unwavering perseverance is his most valuable lesson. His consistent efforts, strategic thinking, and ability to rise above adversity make Swarajya not just history, but a timeless inspiration for all of us.

CHAPTER SIXTEEN

Competition as an Opportunity for Success

Competition is an inevitable part of life, from nature's ecosystems to human society. It exists in every field, profession, and even mundane activities. The presence of competition can seem intimidating, but it also offers immense opportunities for growth and innovation. How we perceive and handle competition determines whether it becomes an obstacle or a stepping stone toward success.

The Universality of Competition

- From Survival to Business:

In nature, survival depends on competition. Whether it's a predator hunting prey or animals vying for territory, competition is fundamental. Similarly, in human life, competition arises when resources are limited—be it in securing a job, succeeding in business, or even something as trivial as finding the best parking spot.

- Competition is Everywhere:

Even in unconventional fields like begging or lying, competition exists. It's not about the field but the mindset you bring to it. Starting a business truthfully? You'll find competitors. Stepping into a field dominated by dishonesty? The competition remains. The key lies in recognizing and adapting to this reality.

Healthy Competition: A Catalyst for Growth

Competition itself is neutral; its impact depends on how we approach it.

1. Perspective Matters:

Viewing competition as a threat breeds insecurity and fear, while seeing it as an opportunity foster learning and resilience.

2. Learning from Competitors:

Competitors can be valuable teachers. Observing their successes and failures offers insights that might take years to discover independently.

3. Avoiding Toxic Rivalry:

Unhealthy competition, marked by envy and hostility, consumes energy that could be used productively. Instead of trying to "eliminate" competitors, focus on improving your own offerings.

No Fixed Formula for Success

Success in a competitive environment doesn't follow a universal blueprint. What works for one business may fail for another. Here's why:

- Diverse Approaches:

Some businesses thrive by prioritizing innovation, while others excel through consistency and reliability.

- Adaptability Over Formula:

Even within the same industry, strategies must adapt to market trends, consumer behaviour, and evolving competition.

Examples of Navigating Competition

1. Restaurants and Customer Loyalty:

Think about local restaurants or food joints you've visited. Some leave a lasting impression with exceptional food and service, while others rely on brand prestige, like luxury hotels. Interestingly, many small eateries maintain their charm and quality for decades, even outshining big chains.

How? Through trust, consistency, and customer relationships.

2. Worker Dedication and Team Spirit:

Successful businesses often owe their longevity to dedicated employees and loyal customers. These establishments don't just survive competition—they thrive because of the trust and collaboration built within their teams.

How to Handle Competitors

1. Learn, Don't Copy:

Competitors can provide a blueprint of what works and what doesn't. Learn from their strategies but avoid imitation. Instead, innovate and improve on their ideas to create something uniquely yours.

2. Focus on Strengths:

Concentrate on what sets you apart. Highlight your unique selling points (USPs) and refine them continuously.

3. Build Relationships:

Cultivating trust with customers and employees often creates a strong foundation that shields businesses from competition. Happy customers are less likely to switch, even if competitors offer lower prices or flashy promotions.

4. Be Adaptable:

Markets change, and so do consumer needs. Staying flexible and ready to evolve is crucial for long-term success.

Competitors as Partners in Growth

Rather than viewing competitors as enemies, consider them collaborators in driving industry standards. Their presence pushes us to:

- Innovate and improve our products or services.
- Stay vigilant and adaptive to market trends.
- Maintain a customer-centric approach, ensuring we don't become complacent.

Competition is not a threat; it's a challenge and an opportunity. By embracing a healthy approach to rivalry, businesses and individuals can grow stronger, more innovative, and better prepared for future challenges. Recognize competitors as teachers and motivators, and use their presence to fuel your journey toward success.

Remember, the goal isn't to eliminate competition—it's to outgrow and outperform it by staying true to your values, adapting to change, and consistently delivering excellence.

Competition as Our Asset: Understanding the Balance in Business

Competition is an undeniable part of life and business. It drives innovation, shapes markets, and challenges us to grow. Instead of fearing or resenting competition, viewing it as an asset allows us to navigate its complexities with wisdom and balance. Let's explore how competition can be turned into a strategic advantage.

The Role of SWOT Analysis

The SWOT (Strengths, Weaknesses, Opportunities, Threats) framework is a powerful tool for evaluating not just our own position but also our competitors'. It requires periodic reassessment to stay relevant in a dynamic business environment.

1. Strengths (S): Identify what makes your business unique. This could be your products, services, or operational efficiency.
2. Weaknesses (W): Recognize areas where you lag and work to improve them without denial or procrastination.

3. Opportunities (O): Spot emerging trends or untapped markets that can propel your business forward.
4. Threats (T): Be vigilant about external risks, including competition, market changes, and economic factors.

However, the key is balance—while assessing competitors is important, losing sight of your own goals and strengths can lead to missteps. Wisdom lies in aligning your analysis with your long-term vision.

The Importance of Balance

In business and life, imbalance often leads to inefficiency and failure. Just as overeating causes indigestion, overfocusing on competitors—or neglecting them entirely—disrupts business health. Balance ensures sustainability and adaptability in the face of challenges.

Many industries today struggle with imbalance, whether in corporate strategies, political agendas, or social policies. While such challenges might seem overwhelming, they're temporary. Nature, with its inherent tendency to restore equilibrium, teaches us that staying aligned with principles of balance and adaptability leads to resilience.

Listening to Criticism with Openness

When starting a business, especially in a circle of family and friends, you'll often encounter scepticism. People may highlight potential pitfalls or share doubts about your decisions. Instead of dismissing their concerns outright, listen carefully:

1. Glean Insights: While criticism might be rooted in negativity, it often contains practical wisdom that can help refine your vision.
2. Stay Focused: Don't let external doubts derail your clarity. Use feedback as a tool to strengthen your resolve rather than as a barrier to progress.

Personal Lessons on Growth and Maturity

Your journey serves as a testament to the power of persistence and practical wisdom. From dealing with unconstructive criticism to valuing the right tools and relationships, your experiences have shaped your outlook on competition and success.

1. Ignoring Unnecessary Criticism: Over time, learning to disregard unsolicited advice and irrelevant judgment helps foster mental clarity and professional maturity.
2. Recognizing the Value of Tools: Early experiences with a Nokia phone in 2004 exemplify how recognizing the importance of tools, even amidst modest circumstances, can lead to growth. Communication became a cornerstone of progress in your life, showing the impact of small, thoughtful investments.
3. The Role of Support in Relationships: Madhuri's practical wisdom and support during challenging times highlighted the value of trust and teamwork. Instead of getting defensive about societal judgments, you both chose humour and practicality—a mature approach to external criticism.

Competition as a Teacher

Rather than treating competitors as adversaries, consider them a source of learning and inspiration:

1. Observe and Adapt: Competitors reveal market gaps and highlight strategies that work. Learn from their successes and mistakes, but don't imitate blindly.
2. Focus on Strengths: Build on your unique qualities while embracing the positive practices of others.
3. Maintain Boundaries: Avoid excessive comparison. While competition is healthy, overindulgence in rivalry drains energy and creativity.

Key Takeaways

- Balance and Wisdom: These are your greatest assets. Whether in competition or personal decisions, maintaining equilibrium leads to sustainable success.

- Criticism as Feedback: Use scepticism as an opportunity for reflection and refinement.
- Learn, Don't Copy: Competitors can inspire growth when approached with the right perspective.
- Focus on Relationships: Trust within your team, and support from loved ones, often determines long-term resilience and success.

Your reflections remind us that maturity and growth come from embracing challenges, staying open to learning, and maintaining focus on one's own path. Competition, far from being a threat, becomes a valuable asset when viewed through the lens of balance and adaptability.

Opportunities in the Franchise Business: A Balanced Perspective

The franchise business offers an attractive opportunity for individuals looking to venture into entrepreneurship without the daunting challenges of building a business from scratch. While competition drives innovation and keeps markets vibrant, franchising provides a structured pathway for those who prefer a guided entry into the business world. However, like any business model, franchising comes with its own set of advantages and limitations that need careful evaluation.

Advantages of Franchising

1. Established Brand Recognition

A significant benefit of franchising is leveraging the reputation of a well-known brand. Customers are more likely to trust and engage with a name they already recognize, reducing the effort and time needed to build credibility in the market.

2. Comprehensive Training and Support

Most franchisors provide detailed training and ongoing support, equipping franchisees with the knowledge to run the business effectively. This can include guidance on operations, staff management, and customer service, laying a strong foundation for success.

3. Shared Marketing and Research

Franchisors handle a significant portion of marketing, product development, and market research at the brand level. This centralized approach reduces the franchisee's burden and costs, offering access to professional strategies and insights.

4. Lower Risk, Proven Systems

Franchising operates on a tried-and-tested business model, reducing the risks associated with starting a business independently. The guidelines and systems in place help minimize errors and provide clarity in operations.

Challenges and Limitations of Franchising

1. Restricted Creativity

Franchisees are required to adhere to the franchisor's policies and practices, leaving limited room for personal innovation or changes. While this ensures consistency across locations, it can feel restrictive for individuals who enjoy creative freedom.

2. High Initial and Ongoing Costs

Franchising involves significant upfront expenses, such as franchise fees and setup costs, as well as ongoing royalty payments. These recurring costs can reduce profit margins, requiring franchisees to manage finances carefully.

3. Dependency on Location and Market

The success of a franchise largely depends on selecting the right location. Poor market research or an oversaturated area can lead to difficulties in attracting customers, even with a strong brand backing.

4. Vulnerability to Brand Reputation

As a franchisee, your business is tied to the franchisor's brand. If the parent company faces negative publicity, financial instability, or policy changes, it can directly impact your business, regardless of your individual performance.

Considerations Before Choosing a Franchise

While the franchise model offers a guided approach to entrepreneurship, it's essential to evaluate its suitability for your goals and circumstances:

- Research Extensively: Understand the franchisor's reputation, market demand, and operational guidelines. Speak with existing franchisees to gain firsthand insights.
- Assess Costs: Calculate both initial investment and ongoing expenses to ensure financial viability.
- Choose the Right Location: Conduct thorough market research to identify a location with high potential for customer demand and minimal competition.
- Understand the Agreement: Review the franchise contract carefully to ensure you are comfortable with the terms, restrictions, and obligations.
- Evaluate Personal Fit: Consider whether the franchise model aligns with your personality and business aspirations. If you value creativity and autonomy, the restrictions of a franchise might feel limiting.

Franchising presents an opportunity for aspiring entrepreneurs to benefit from an established business model while mitigating some risks of starting a business independently. However, it is not a one-size-fits-all solution. By understanding the balance between its advantages and challenges, individuals can make informed decisions that align with their goals, financial capacity, and vision for success. A thoughtful and strategic approach to franchising can pave the way for a fulfilling and prosperous business journey.

Understanding MLM (Multi-Level Marketing): A Cautious Perspective

Multi-Level Marketing (MLM) has gained significant popularity in recent years, with companies like Amway, Herbalife, Vestige, and Modicare leading the charge. While some individuals have experienced financial success through MLM, the industry is rife with controversy and scepticism due to frequent cases of fraud and exploitation.

MLM operates on a pyramid-like structure where participants earn commissions by selling products and recruiting others into the system. The appeal lies in the promise of earning substantial passive income through network growth. However, this model has also been exploited by fraudulent schemes that target vulnerable individuals, particularly in rural areas and smaller cities.

The Dark Side of MLM

1. Fraudulent Companies

History is littered with examples of MLM companies that have defrauded millions, such as Pearless, Pan Card Club, PACL, and Nmart. These companies lure people with promises of high returns—often unrealistic, such as a 10% monthly interest—only to collapse and leave investors in financial ruin.

2. False Promises of Wealth

While MLM success stories exist, they are often the exception rather than the rule. A handful of individuals at the top of the pyramid enjoy significant earnings, often flaunting luxury items like Mercedes or BMWs. However, the vast majority of participants end up wasting their time and money, unable to achieve similar success.

3. Impact on the Middle Class

Many MLM schemes target the middle class, offering seemingly easy ways to supplement income. Educated individuals and professionals have also fallen prey, enticed by promises of quick wealth. Despite regular warnings and reports of fraud, these schemes continue to proliferate.

The MLM Model vs. Independent Business

Multilevel Marketing (MLM) and traditional industry or business models differ significantly across various components. In terms of financial investment, MLM usually requires low or no upfront capital, making it accessible for individuals without substantial resources. On the other hand, starting an industry or a business typically demands a significant financial investment, especially when aiming for large-scale operations.

When it comes to profit generation, MLM income heavily depends on the growth of one's network. Initially, the earnings are often low, but they can increase significantly with a strong and expanding downline. Conversely, traditional businesses might experience losses or negative profits during the early stages. However, with consistent effort, strategic planning, and business growth, they can yield substantial profits over time.

Regarding independence, MLM participants have limited freedom since they must operate within the company's predefined policies and structures. In contrast, business owners enjoy greater independence, with more flexibility in decision-making and the ability to craft their own strategies.

Risk is another major differentiator. MLM involves a high risk of time loss and potential damage to personal reputation, although the monetary risk is generally lower. In business or industry, the risks are more substantial—both financially and operationally—and require effective risk management strategies to ensure long-term sustainability.

Lastly, the skills required for success in MLM focus primarily on sales and networking. Meanwhile, running a business or operating in the industry demands a broader skill set, including planning, execution, sales, and customer relationship management, among others.

Key Takeaways

1. Understand the Reality

MLM is not a guaranteed path to wealth. While the initial investment may seem low, the true cost often lies in wasted time, strained relationships, and missed opportunities to pursue more sustainable ventures.

2. Evaluate Carefully

If you are considering joining an MLM, research the company thoroughly. Understand the products, compensation structure, and the experiences of others who have participated. Be wary of schemes that promise extraordinary returns with minimal effort.

3. Focus on Independent Growth

Running an independent business offers greater control, creativity, and potential for long-term success. While it requires higher investment and involves more risk, the rewards are often more fulfilling and sustainable.

4. Avoid Exploitative Systems

Avoid schemes that prey on others' ignorance or desperation. If a business opportunity feels too good to be true, it likely is. Ethical and sustainable practices should always be prioritized.

While MLM may seem like an easy entry point into the business world, it is essential to approach it with caution. The industry's track record of fraud and exploitation underscores the need for thorough evaluation and scepticism. On the other hand, building an independent business requires more effort but offers genuine opportunities for growth and fulfillment. Ultimately, the choice lies in aligning your goals with a path that prioritizes ethics, sustainability, and personal satisfaction.

Business is About Strong Theory and Effective Execution

Growing a business isn't just about having a big idea—it's about turning that idea into reality through disciplined execution. Many times, we assume that just having clarity of vision is enough for success. But in reality, execution is the key factor that separates dreamers from achievers.

A real-life example from my own school days comes to mind. He wasn't my classmate, but I've observed his journey for over 25 years. It wouldn't be appropriate to name him here, but his story is worth sharing.

Back in school, he was known for his carefree attitude. Coming from a poor background, with no father and a mother who worked tirelessly, he seemed least concerned about studies. He spent most of his time playing cricket, gilli-danda, and wandering aimlessly. While the rest of us followed a disciplined school routine, he seemed completely detached from any structured life.

He was the kind of boy who would go without a bath for 15 days straight, earning both our ridicule and admiration for his carefree nature.

Years later, I saw him again while visiting some relatives. By then, he had a small hardware stall at the bus stand. It wasn't much, but he was making progress. Over time, I kept hearing about how his business was growing steadily.

While I was working jobs, caught in life's endless cycle of responsibilities, he had transformed his small shop into a full-fledged hardware business. Today, that once carefree boy is a respected businessman.

There was a time when people doubted if he would ever settle down, but today, he has built a strong business and a stable family life. Every time we pass his shop, my wife jokingly reminds me—*"Look, there's your friend who once hated taking baths, now running a thriving business."* We honk, wave, and continue on our way.

His journey, from poverty to financial success, is true inspiration. Many of us look up to billionaires as role models, but often, true entrepreneurial lessons can be found in the people around us. Their stories remind us that success is not about where you start, but how you move forward.

This is the reason I wrote this book to highlight real-life entrepreneurial journeys and inspire others.

Building a Business Requires Proven Theories and Frameworks

Business is not just gut instinct; it is also about applying tested strategies and theories. Over time, several business models have shaped industries, and they continue to offer valuable lessons.

One of the most well-known theories is SWOT Analysis (Strengths, Weaknesses, Opportunities, and Threats). It helps businesses assess their position in the market and identify areas for growth.

Another powerful concept is Porter's Five Forces Model, developed by Michael Porter. He identified five key elements that determine market competition and business success:

1. Industry Rivalry – Understanding your competition
2. Threat of New Entrants – Assessing how easy it is for new businesses to enter your market
3. Bargaining Power of Suppliers – Managing supplier relationships effectively
4. Bargaining Power of Buyers – Keeping customers loyal while offering value
5. Threat of Substitutes – Identifying alternative products that could disrupt your business

One of my favourite theories is The Lean Startup Model by Eric Ries. He emphasizes the MVP (Minimum Viable Product) approach—meaning, instead of overcomplicating business ideas, start with a basic version of your product or service, test it in the market, gather feedback, and then improve accordingly.

This method ensures that you don't waste excessive time and money on building something customers may not want. The model also stresses the importance of pivoting—if your idea doesn't work, either change direction or refine your approach instead of persisting with a failing strategy.

Another important business framework is Maslow's Hierarchy of Needs, which explains how consumer psychology influences purchasing decisions. It categorizes customer needs into:

- Basic needs (food, water, shelter)
- Safety needs (financial security, health)
- Social needs (relationships, community)
- Esteem needs (recognition, status)
- Self-actualization (personal growth and fulfillment)

This is crucial for businesses, as it helps them understand consumer behaviour and position their products accordingly.

Similarly, Consumer Psychology & Brand Loyalty Theory highlights how businesses should focus on building trust, emotional connections, and high-quality service to retain customers.

The Pareto Principle (80/20 Rule), proposed by Vilfredo Pareto, states that 80% of a company's revenue comes from 20% of its customers. This means businesses should focus on their most valuable customers and ensure they stay loyal.

Business is a Mindset, Not Just a Profit-Making Activity

A business isn't just about chasing profits—it's about developing a sustainable vision. It requires deep thought, strategic execution, and a positive impact on society.

Success in business isn't just numbers; it's about building something meaningful and lasting. If our business philosophy is positive and ethical, our profits will be sustainable.

Ultimately, business success isn't just about revenue figures—it's about long-term impact, stability, and continuous learning. Everything else is just statistics.

CHAPTER SEVENTEEN

Get Set Grow

As I wrap up this exploration of business and industry, I find myself reflecting on the idea that a page never truly ends. Much like an ongoing saga, the journey of business is ever- evolving, and there are always new lessons to learn, new strategies to implement, and new challenges to overcome. This narrative is just one chapter in an ever-expanding book of knowledge.

In my attempt to share my understanding of business, I know there are aspects I have left out, and that's okay. As with anything in life, there will always be more to learn, more to contribute, and more to refine. I may revisit these ideas in future editions, incorporating fresh perspectives and the wisdom gained from experience. However, for now, I wish to leave you with a few points for reflection, hoping they will help guide you as you venture forward.

The phrase "Get Set Grow" symbolizes more than just a call to action; it embodies the spirit of readiness, resilience, and growth. In business, we must always be prepared for the journey ahead, setting clear goals and staying focused. Success, when it comes, should never make us complacent or arrogant. The world around us will constantly test us, and challenges will emerge as part of the journey. But rather than asking "Why me?" when difficulties arise, we must shift our mindset to, "What can I learn from this?" Every obstacle presents an opportunity for growth and a chance to refine our approach.

It is essential to understand that true change doesn't come from the cries of the oppressed but from the thoughtful strategies and actions of victorious leaders. As we navigate the ups and downs of business, we must keep our focus on bringing about positive change, not just for ourselves but for society as a whole. In times of adversity, remember that success isn't just about personal achievement—it's about contributing to the greater good.

I think of the example of prominent industrialists, such as Gautam Adani and Elon Musk, who, despite facing significant challenges, continue to make waves in their respective industries. Whether or not the media reports about them are entirely true, their influence and reach are undeniable. Their journeys remind us that as we pursue our business ambitions, we must be prepared to face challenges that might come from all sides—whether from competitors, the public, or even the very systems that govern us.

In business, we must be ready for these challenges, but we must also do so with a sense of ethics. Business strategies often involve persuasion, negotiation, and sometimes even compromise. But it's crucial to remember that while we may not always be able to operate with perfect ethics, we should strive to keep a minimum level of ethical conduct in our practices. Our actions should always aim to benefit society, even as we work toward professional success. It's about finding that balance—ensuring that our growth does not come at the cost of others' well-being.

As we grow our businesses, it's vital that our strategies support not just our personal success, but the collective health and well-being of the communities we serve. When we aim for growth in a sustainable way—one that respects others, promotes social welfare, and considers the long-term impact—we set ourselves on a path of lasting success. The health of our businesses, our society, and our minds are interconnected, and it is only through ethical business practices and mindful strategies that we can maintain that balance.

As you set out on your own business journey, remember this: Success requires preparation, resilience, and an unwavering commitment to growth. Stay ethical, stay focused, and let your actions shape not just your success, but a better world for everyone around you.

Wisdom Leads to Maturity

The essence of building any successful business lies in understanding the needs of the customer, developing innovative ideas, maintaining trustworthiness, executing precise strategies, and fostering teamwork. However, to ensure these elements come together effectively, there is one quality that must be embedded in us: wisdom. Wisdom is not an innate quality; it isn't something we're born with. Even among communities often recognized for their entrepreneurial spirit—such as the Jains, Marwaris, Gujaratis, or Sindhis—wisdom is not an automatic trait. It needs to be cultivated over time.

While knowledge provides the foundation, wisdom is what directs that knowledge towards effective and meaningful action. Wisdom is born from life experiences—through trials, challenges, and the insights gained from overcoming them. It is wisdom that helps us make accurate, well-informed decisions, particularly when it comes to managing risks or handling stressful situations. With wisdom comes composure. This quality allows us to navigate uncertainties calmly, making decisions based on sound judgment rather than impulsive reactions.

It is important to note that wisdom is not a static trait. It doesn't simply appear after years of study or experience. Even after we've acquired wisdom, it must continue to grow and evolve. It is a continuous process, fuelled by an openness to learn. This is how we develop maturity, which I believe is the real gem of life. Maturity is not something we achieve once and for all; it is a lifelong process of growth, refinement, and learning.

We Must Give Up Ego and Arrogance

To walk the path of wisdom and maturity, we must rid ourselves of certain vices, particularly ego and arrogance. These two are often at the core of many failures, and no one is immune to them. We've all heard that one should have self-confidence and a sense of pride in one's achievements, but it's crucial to recognize the fine line between healthy self-respect and the toxic forces of ego and arrogance.

In truth, ego is the root cause of arrogance. When we let go of our ego, we automatically rid ourselves of the arrogance that stems from it. Ego tends to blind us to opportunities for growth and learning. We may become fixated on proving ourselves or protecting our reputation, often at the cost of real progress. I've seen highly intelligent and knowledgeable people fall into this trap. Their egos, fuelled by jealousy and envy, eventually led them to failure. It is the very desire to be seen as superior that holds them back from evolving or collaborating with others.

I have personally witnessed the consequences of holding on to one's ego. For example, a friend of mine spent seven crucial years struggling to secure a road for a poultry farm he had built. His stubbornness and ego wouldn't allow him to take a step back, even when it was clear that his efforts were not yielding the desired results. This ego-driven determination cost him valuable time and opportunities. In contrast, another friend—despite having a legal claim to a piece of land and a house—chose to sell the property and leave, knowing that it would bring him peace and open new doors. Today, this friend is thriving, while the former remains stuck in his ego-driven battle.

Throughout life, many people will try to pull you into a web of competition. They will put up obstacles at every turn, trying to distract you from your goal. It's your choice whether to succumb to these distractions or rise above them. Think of the story of Abhimanyu in the Mahabharata, trapped in the Chakravyuha, a complex military formation. He fought valiantly but ultimately became ensnared. In business, we face similar challenges—obstacles that seem insurmountable or traps that we cannot avoid. In these moments, it's important to remember that having a guide, someone like Krishna, can make all the difference. With the right guidance, we won't lose our direction or get caught in unnecessary conflicts.

The lesson here is simple: let go of ego, embrace wisdom, and find the humility to learn and grow continuously. Only then can we navigate the challenges of business and life with composure, clarity, and maturity.

The World is Much Bigger Than Our Ego or Arrogance

The world we live in is far greater than the confines of our ego or arrogance. Positive and practical thoughts have far more significance than the distractions created by our inflated self-image. Unfortunately, many individuals waste valuable time and resources getting entangled in these unnecessary pursuits. There is an old piece of wisdom from our ancestors, which advises against stepping into a court or police station without a valid reason. This advice serves as a reminder that many dreams are derailed by unnecessary conflicts and entanglements.

That said, this doesn't mean we should be 100% fearful or spineless in the face of challenges. It simply means we should remain calm, set aside ego, and approach such situations wisely. When faced with challenges, it's important to remain composed and take the right actions when the time comes. If we can act strategically and with humility, we might even catch others off guard, giving us an edge in difficult situations.

Our Indian mythological stories are a great source of such lessons. These stories are not random tales but are full of deep insights. For instance, the epics Ramayana and Mahabharata are not just historical accounts but monumental works that teach us how to live our lives practically and wisely.

These texts offer more than mere religious teachings; they are filled with strategies for overcoming personal struggles, leadership, and ethical decision-making.

To truly understand these teachings, we must engage with them ourselves, not merely rely on external sermons or kirtans. The essence of these ancient stories can only be grasped through personal reflection, reading, and comprehension.

Practical Wisdom for Growth

In business and in life, it is crucial to expand our understanding through practical means. Growth doesn't come from superficial knowledge or trivial distractions, but from serious contemplation, meditation, reading, and real-world experience. One important lesson is that we should not be afraid to make mistakes. Mistakes are part of growth. What matters is learning from them and using those lessons to refine our approach.

As we move forward in business, we need to carefully assess what we must shed and what we should hold on to in order to ensure growth. This requires a mindset of humility, the ability to discard ego, and an open mind to learn from others. I once read an insightful article by Shrikant Avhad on the "Entrepreneur Friends" Facebook page, where he talked about how many of us feel inferior or embarrassed when seeking guidance from others, especially peers or acquaintances. This often stems from our ego, which keeps us from asking for help when we need it the most.

In today's world, there's a noticeable shift where the focus has moved away from valuing genuine knowledge and education. Instead, political leaders and religious figures often dominate public attention, while those who make real contributions in fields like science, writing, or social service receive less recognition. This imbalance in society affects our collective growth and understanding.

A Conversation on Society's Focus

I once had a conversation with a friend who cynically remarked, "You only like to talk about religion and politics. Everyone has their importance in society. You see the world through your own lens and try to show it to us." To this, I responded, "Imagine if, in a single day in Ahmednagar (now Ahilyanagar), there is a program with the Prime Minister and Chief

Minister, followed by an event with political leaders, a religious conference, an election campaign, and a musical performance. Now, imagine that alongside these, there's also a book fair, an art exhibition, a professional guidance seminar, or a session with world-renowned social workers or scientists from ISRO and Bhabha Institute. What will the people of our society attend? What will they prioritize?"

My friend was unable to answer, and his face fell, as he realized the truth. The point is that we always have a choice in how we prioritize our time and energy. The decision about where we direct our attention can greatly influence our growth.

The Choice Is Ours

The choice is ours, and it is not about opposing every good initiative, but rather deciding what truly matters. In the example above, it's clear that while political, religious, or cultural events may draw attention, we must prioritize intellectual, scientific, and professional growth. When we focus on our true goals and protect ourselves from distractions, we pave the way for real progress.

There was a time when my pursuit of knowledge led me to social isolation. My constant focus on learning distanced me from many people in my village. However, looking back now, it is they who no longer seek my company. This was a difficult but necessary phase. There were times when I tried to explain basic ethics and practical wisdom to others, but their focus was on material gains and status. I watched as younger individuals became 'youth leaders' or 'business tycoons,' flaunting cars and gold rings while I remained focused on deeper, more meaningful goals.

But here's the key: ignore the distractions. Don't let your ego be bruised just because others overlook you or prioritize superficial things. Continue with your work sincerely and loyally, and success will eventually come. It's through this persistence and focus that the world will eventually see the goodness in you—or at least appreciate what you've tried to achieve. For this, we must learn to value our time and money wisely, for they are the resources that will propel us forward in our journey toward growth and success.

Ego Growth with Success and Wealth

As we achieve success or accumulate wealth, our ego tends to grow. In my earlier years, I used to believe that a person should be proud of their education and knowledge rather than their money. Now, I realize the folly of that thinking. Just like we should not be proud of our caste or religion—because these are not factors, we earned or chose—we should not take pride in wealth, knowledge, or education. Instead, education and knowledge should humble us, diminishing our ego, pride, and arrogance. Wealth should not make us feel superior; rather, it should increase our sense of responsibility.

When we accumulate wealth, it's important to remember that we are not the true owners of the money or institutions we manage; we are merely trustees. By viewing our wealth through this lens, we foster a sense of duty and responsibility that nurtures growth. Only by recognizing this can we achieve sustainable success, maintain peace of mind, and ensure that our success isn't fleeting. True inner peace comes from understanding our role as caretakers of the wealth we have, not as its owners.

Avoid Getting Trapped in Shortcuts

In today's world, how money is earned seems less important than how much one has. This shift in focus has led to a decline in values such as social integrity, ethics, loyalty, and a sense of duty. Much like politics once suggested abandoning these values to achieve success, this mindset has now spread to social and economic activities as well. Quick-money-making schemes, such as Ponzi schemes, are thriving as a result. These schemes are being promoted by multicity or multistate institutions that are spreading rapidly, deceiving many. Similarly, fraudulent activities like stock market scams, under the guise of "investment opportunities," are also rampant.

Some institutions, operating from places like Mumbai and Navi Mumbai, now teach people how to deceive others. These individuals are preying on vulnerable entrepreneurs and young people, enticing them into business dealings that are unethical and ultimately damaging. I have witnessed such scams firsthand, particularly in the Nagar and Marathwada regions, where many young people are falling into these traps because they are attracted to the idea of quick wealth. It's critical to avoid these shortcuts in business and remain true to ethical and honest practices.

Shortcuts in Business

In business, shortcuts often appear like tempting lollipops, offering an easy path to quick rewards. These shortcuts may seem appealing, especially when the temptation of rapid success is hard to resist. I too have faced these temptations in my career. However, thanks to the practical and thoughtful friends around me, I never strayed from the path of integrity and careful planning. Success in business is never a straight highway. There will always be distractions and shortcuts trying to pull you in, but they rarely lead to lasting success.

Even if, by some fluke, a shortcut brings you temporary success, it's likely to be short- lived. Take the example of schemes like "Sahyadri" or "BHR Co-operative" or even "KBC." These were all classic cases of Ponzi schemes. Not only did they collapse, but the vendors, representatives, and investors all lost their money. Despite the collapse of so many similar schemes, I continue to be astonished by how the middle-class society still falls for such fraudulent schemes. In our Nagar district, for instance, it is common to find that at least six out of every ten families have either been cheated in the past or are currently being scammed.

The reality is that shortcuts may provide temporary gains, but in the long run, they only bring harm to everyone involved. So, avoid these deceptive paths. Stick to your strategic plans, work diligently, and stay true to ethical principles. Only through perseverance and integrity will you achieve lasting success.

The Shortcut Myth in Business

In today's world, many dream of becoming crorepatis (millionaires) in a matter of months, driving luxury cars like Audis or Thars, and showing off their success. I am frequently approached by individuals asking for tips on how to make quick and easy money. Over time, I have stopped giving such advice because I realized the futility of it. It's like trying to pour water into a broken vessel—no matter how much you try, it just won't hold. There are limits to what you can do, and business is not about quick fixes or shortcuts.

An entrepreneur or businessman never seeks shortcuts. Those who chase these shortcuts are not genuine entrepreneurs. Business is about building a strong foundation and growing steadily. If the foundation is weak or non-existent, the results will be unsatisfactory, like a house without solid ground beneath it. Every business demands patience, courage, and continuous learning. Success in business comes from study, strategy, experience, and most importantly, the trust of customers. These are the real keys to success, and the satisfaction comes from the process, not from instant gains. In the end, how much money you make, what turnover you achieve, or how lavish your lifestyle becomes should be secondary to the meaningful work you are doing and the impact you're creating.

Striving for a Positive Business Culture

I feel truly inspired whenever I discuss business practices with my colleagues and mentors, Yogesh Katare and Kishore Raktate, from my AVGC team. They focus on more than just economic statistics; their main goal is nurturing social welfare and finding satisfaction in the work itself. They are masters at guiding others to create a positive business culture. Every time I interact with them, I come away with a renewed sense of purpose and fulfillment.

Success in business is never just about individual effort—it's a result of collective work, shared knowledge, and the aggregation of good decisions. Both Yogesh and Kishore emphasize the importance of work culture. Now, in my forties, I understand its significance more deeply. Even if you are highly intelligent, without a strong, positive business culture, challenges will arise. Tata Group stands as a prime example of a strong work culture. Globally, writings about their ideals are celebrated, and their work culture is a benchmark. Even wealthy companies, no matter how successful their leadership, often seem inferior compared to Tata's culture.

If we want to experience true satisfaction in business, we need to build a business model that is socially aware and oriented toward well-being. Otherwise, we are simply participating in a numbers game—playing a wild game of rummy with no long-term purpose.

Building Trust and Unity in the Workplace

In our small organization, my wife, Madhuri, implemented a policy three years ago to give female employees at least one paid leave day each month for their menstrual cycle. I was immediately supportive of this idea, and we continue to implement it today. Additionally, when employees take leave due to illness, we do not deduct their salaries. It may seem like a small gesture, but these decisions have contributed significantly to building team unity and trust.

I can make such decisions because I have personally experienced exploitation. In my early days, I worked in a forging company in Supa MIDC and witnessed the struggles of labourers in the journalism industry across Pune, Mumbai, and later, Ahmednagar. This exposure removed the divide between workers and employers from my mind. Today, our organization's policy is simple: seniority and hierarchy should exist only to facilitate work. It should not be a barrier to equal treatment or respect.

I believe that everyone, regardless of their position, should be treated with the same respect and understanding. Our work culture reflects this. We understand how crucial it is to maintain professionalism for smooth, trustworthy relationships within the organization. By focusing on fairness, we create a work environment that fosters cooperation and growth.

Concluding Thoughts and Continuous Improvement

Now, I conclude this discussion, having shared everything that has been on my mind. However, there are many issues that I haven't touched upon, such as business health or accounting, and other scientifically structured aspects of business. These are not areas I feel equipped to speak about, and I didn't intend for this conversation to focus on them. Still, I welcome any suggestions and guidance you might have on these topics, as I aim to improve in future editions.

Change is an ongoing process, and those like me, who believe in it as a core value, understand that it is essential to growth. The individual who embraces change and works towards continual improvement is the one who moves toward success. On the other hand, those who resist change and remain stagnant know well what happens after that.